THE YUKON &
NORTHWEST
TERRITORIES

D1556078

ANDREW HEMPSTEAD

Contents

The Yukon 7
Planning Your Time............... 10

The Southeast 10
Watson Lake 10
  ◖ Signpost Forest................... 11
  Other Sights 11
  Accommodations and Camping 12
  Food 12
Watson Lake to Whitehorse....... 12
  Teslin 12
  Teslin to Whitehorse............... 13
Atlin............................ 13
  Sights 13
  Practicalities 13
Carcross and Vicinity 13
  Sights 14
  Accommodations and Food......... 14

Whitehorse...................... 14
  History 14
Sights........................... 16
  ◖ SS *Klondike* 16
  MacBride Museum 16
  Yukon Beringia Interpretive Centre... 16
  Yukon Transportation Museum 17
  Schwatka Lake and Miles Canyon 18
  Takhini Hot Springs 18
Recreation 18
  Historical and Nature Walks 18
  ◖ Dog-Mushing 19
  Biking and Golf 19
Shopping 19
  Bookstores........................ 19
Entertainment and Events 20
  Festivals and Events................20

Accommodations and Camping...20
Food.............................. 21
Information 22
Getting There 22
Getting Around.................... 23

Whitehorse
to Beaver Creek 23
  Whitehorse to Haines Junction 23
Haines Junction.................. 23
  Sights............................ 23
  Accommodations and Camping 24
  Food 24
  Information 24
◖ Kluane National Park..........24
  The Land 24
  Flightseeing...................... 25
  Tours............................. 25
  Practicalities 25
Haines Junction to
Beaver Creek.................... 25
  Destruction Bay 26
  Burwash Landing 26
Beaver Creek..................... 26
  Accommodations and Food.......... 26
  Information 26
  Onward to Alaska 26

Whitehorse
to Dawson City 27
  Lake Laberge 27
  Carmacks.......................... 27
  Five Finger Rapids 27
  Pelly Crossing 27
  Silver Trail 27

Dawson City 28

History.........................28
Gold Fever 28
Heyday and Pay Dirt 30

Sights..........................30
◖ Dawson City Museum............30
SS *Keno* 31
◖ Dawson Historical Complex
    National Historic Site............ 31
Robert Service Cabin............... 31
Midnight Dome 31
◖ The Gold Fields 31

Entertainment 32

Shopping.......................33

Accommodations and Camping...33

Food............................35

Information 35

Getting There 35

Continuing West to Alaska 35
Top of the World Highway..........36

Northwest Territories..37
Planning Your Time..............38

Waterfalls Route.............40

60th Parallel to Hay River.......40
Twin Falls Gorge Territorial Park 40

Hay River 40
Sights 41
Recreation.......................42
Accommodations and Camping 43
Food 43
Information 43
Getting There 43

Hay River to Fort Smith 43
Fort Resolution...................43
Continuing to Fort Smith
    on Highway 5 44

Fort Smith 44
Sights 44
Accommodations and Camping 45

◖ **Wood Buffalo National Park** ...45
Sights 46
Practicalities 47

Hay River to Yellowknife.........47
Lady Evelyn Falls Territorial Park.....47
Fort Providence 47
Rae-Edzo 47

Yellowknife....................48
History 48

Sights..........................48
◖ Prince of Wales
    Northern Heritage Centre........48
Legislative Assembly of
    the Northwest Territories........48
◖ Old Town.......................50
Ingraham Trail....................50
Fred Henne Territorial Park 50

Recreation 50
Fishing and Canoeing...............50
◖ Golfing Under the Midnight Sun... 51

Nightlife........................ 51

Festivals and Events 51

Accommodations and Camping... 51

Food............................52

Information 52
Libraries and Bookstores 52

Services........................53

Getting There 53

Getting Around.................53

Nahanni Country and
    the Mackenzie Valley.......53
West to Fort Simpson 53
Sambaa Deh Falls Territorial Park 53

Fort Simpson....................54
  Sights and Recreation 54
  Accommodations and Food..........55
  Information and Services 55

Liard Highway....................55
  Blackstone Territorial Park..........55

Fort Liard 55
  Birchbark Baskets..................55
  Practicalities 55

◖ **Nahanni National Park** 56
  History............................56
  The Land 56
  Running the South Nahanni
    with an Outfitter.................56
  Your Own White-Water Expedition....57
  Flightseeing......................57
  Information 57

**Towns Along the
  Mackenzie River** 57
  Wrigley...........................58
  Norman Wells 58
  Canol Heritage Trail................58
  Tulita.............................59
  Great Bear Lake 59

Fort Good Hope....................59
Colville Lake 59

Western Arctic................60

Inuvik 60
  Sights............................60
  Tours.............................61
  Festivals and Events...............61
  Accommodations and Camping 61
  Food 63
  Information and Services 63
  Getting There and Around 63

Aklavik..........................63
  Tours.............................63

◖ **Tuktoyaktuk**...................64
  Sights............................64
  Practicalities 64

Paulatuk 64
  Practicalities 64

Banks Island 65
  Sachs Harbour (Ikaahuk)............65

Ulukhaktok.......................65
  Practicalities 65

THE YUKON & NORTHWEST TERRITORIES

THE YUKON

The Yukon sits like a great upside-down wedge—bordered by Alaska, British Columbia, Northwest Territories, and the Arctic Ocean—at the north corner of western Canada. Wilderness and history enriched by the Klondike gold rush combine to create a unique destination, very different from the rest of the country, but easily accessible by plane or by the Alaska Highway. The massive St. Elias Mountains pass through the territory's southwest corner, while the rest of the Yukon is a huge expanse of rolling hills, long narrow lakes, and boreal forests that give way to rolling tundra north of the Arctic Circle. Through the heart of it all flows the Yukon River. Wildlife is present in amazing numbers: 300,000 caribou, 50,000 moose, 22,000 Dall and Stone sheep, 10,000 black bears, 7,000 grizzlies, 4,500 wolves, and 2,000 mountain goats.

The territorial human population is just 31,000, almost 75 percent of them living in the capital, Whitehorse. One of the world's largest northern cities, this bustling city is filled with gold rush history, but is also a great place to soak up city luxuries before heading into the wilderness. In addition to modern hotels, Whitehorse boats a couple of golf courses, great biking and canoeing, good food, and an unexpected surprise, simply divine coffee roasted within city limits. From the capital, the Alaska Highway draws many road warriors farther west, passing by the magnificent wilderness of Kluane National Park before jogging north to Alaska. The Klondike Highway runs 536 kilometers (333 miles) from Whitehorse to Dawson City, site of the world's most frenzied gold rush. The

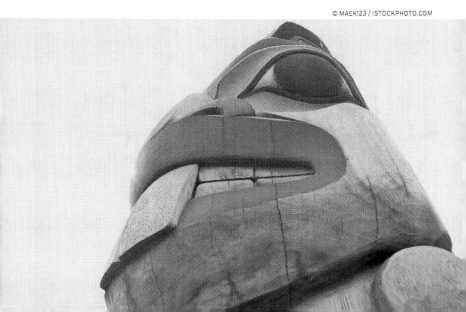

HIGHLIGHTS

◖ **Signpost Forest:** The first attraction north of the border is a little bit corny, but with an interesting history and thousands of town signs to look at, it's a good place to stretch your legs (page 11).

◖ **SS *Klondike*:** Step aboard one of the grandest stern-wheelers ever to ply the waters of the Yukon River (page 16).

◖ **Dog-Mushing:** A summertime visit to the kennels of Frank Turner will give you a taste of what winter brings. And if you are visiting in winter, there's the opportunity to try the pastime yourself (page 19).

◖ **Kluane National Park:** This park may border the Alaska Highway, but plan on hiking

or canoeing to soak up this northern wilderness in all of its raw beauty (page 24).

◖ **Dawson City Museum:** This museum should be the starting point of a walking tour through the infamous mining town – worth the price of admission for the mining-history displays alone (page 30).

◖ **Dawson Historical Complex National Historic Site:** A walk through Dawson City leads past all of Dawson's most important and distinctive historic buildings, now protected as a National Historic Site (page 31).

◖ **The Gold Fields:** Once you've seen Dawson City, get out into the actual gold fields – and even try your hand at panning for gold (page 31).

LOOK FOR ◖ TO FIND RECOMMENDED SIGHTS, ACTIVITIES, DINING, AND LODGING.

trip north from Whitehorse along the Yukon River follows the same route taken by thousands of stampeders in the late 1890s, except instead of riverboats it's RVs and rental cars filled with modern-day travelers in search of adventure. Parks Canada and the Klondike Visitors Association (KVA) have been doing an outstanding job bringing the color of life

back to Dawson City. Many ramshackle buildings have been spruced up with brightly painted facades and informative window displays, and most of the commercial hotels, gift shops, restaurants, beauty parlors, bed-and-breakfasts, and other businesses have followed suit. Thankfully, much of the semi–ghost town flavor remains.

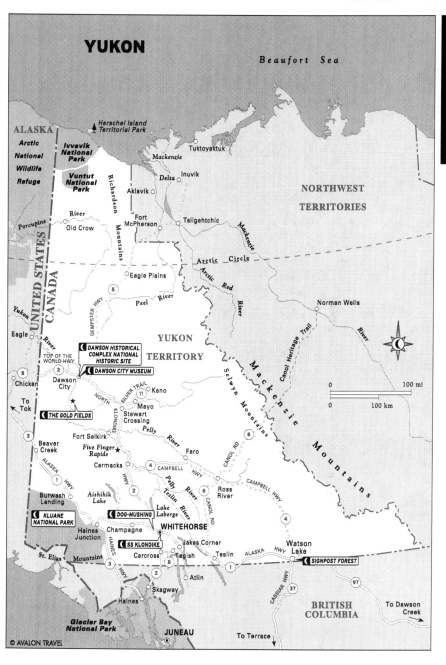

© AVALON TRAVEL

PLANNING YOUR TIME

The Yukon is a destination in itself, with some excellent packages offered by the local airline, Air North (867/668-2228, www.flyairnorth.com), that include airfares from the southern gateways of Vancouver, Edmonton, and Calgary, as well as accommodations and the option of traveling one-way in a rented campervan.

If you want to get a taste of the far north and only have a few days, these deals are the best option. For those driving, allow at least two full, long days to reach Watson Lake from either Vancouver or Edmonton. Add in a minimum of five days in the Yukon along with the return day and you have a nine-day excursion. For the amount of driving involved, this isn't a very practical option and therefore you should allow at least two weeks from the southern gateways. You don't necessarily need to use this extra time in the Yukon, but it allows the opportunity to break up highway time with leisurely stops in northern or central British Columbia, or to include a loop through the southern Northwest Territories. But the most popular way to include the Yukon in a two-week itinerary is to travel one-way by ferry down Alaska's Inside Passage. You can use BC Ferries (www.bcferries.com) to travel up the British Columbia coast as far as Prince Rupert, from where the Alaska Marine Highway System

(www.dot.state.ak.us/amhs) delivers travelers as far north as Skagway and Haines, both an hour's drive from the Yukon.

Why should you travel all this way? Sure there are official "sights," but the purpose of your trip should be primarily to experience wilderness in its most pristine form, in officially designated areas such as Kluane National Park—canoeing across a lake at dawn, soaking in hot springs, or viewing the abundant wildlife. That said, almost everyone makes a stop at the Signpost Forest in Watson Lake, and then spends a day exploring the history of Whitehorse at attractions like the SS *Klondike*. In winter, dog-mushing is becoming big tourism business, but even in summer, visiting the kennels of a racer like Frank Turner will give you a taste of this exiting sport.

From Whitehorse, it's an easy day's drive north to Dawson City, where you should plan to spend at least two days. Dawson City Museum encapsulates the history of this infamous mining town in one building, but to experience the real Dawson, you want to spend the rest of the day on foot visiting the Dawson Historical Complex National Historic Site and a half-day exploring the nearby Gold Fields, where at least one company offers the chance to try gold-panning, and where you can even stay overnight in a traditional wall tent.

The Southeast

The **Alaska Highway** (Alcan) crosses into the Yukon some 1,000 kilometers (620 miles) northwest of Dawson Creek, then ducks back in and out of British Columbia a couple more times before crossing into the Yukon again and reaching the highway town of Watson Lake. From this point, travelers either continue east to the territorial capital or complete the loop through northern British Columbia by taking the Cassiar Highway (Hwy. 37) south to Meziadin Junction.

Over the years, the Alaska Highway has been shortened by straightening some sections

and cutting out big bends completely. Mileage posts in British Columbia have been replaced to reflect these new distances, but those on the Yukon side haven't—so you'll see a 40-kilometer (25-mile) discrepancy beyond the border.

WATSON LAKE

This is the first town in Yukon Territory for all drivers heading north from British Columbia. Even though it's not pretty, it's a welcome sight after the several hundred kilometers on the Cassiar Highway or the all-day ride from Fort Nelson on the Alaska Highway.

Originally inhabited by Kaska Indians, Watson Lake (the town) was created to serve one of a string of airfields constructed across northern Canada in 1940, and its existence was ensured when the Alcan was routed through to service the airfield. Today Watson Lake functions as the hub of a large area of southern Yukon, southwestern Northwest Territories, and northern British Columbia. With a population of 1,500, it's the third largest town in the territory.

◖ Signpost Forest

The famous Signpost Forest originated in 1942 by a G.I. working on the highway who, when given the task of repainting the road's directional sign, added the direction and mileage to his hometown of Danville, Illinois. Since then, more than 40,000 other signs have been added to the collection with town signs, license plates, posters, pie tins, gold-panning pans, mufflers, driftwood, even flywheels stating where the contributor is from and who he/she is. You can put up your addition personally or take it inside to the adjacent **Watson Lake Visitor**

Information Centre (corner of Alaska Hwy. and Robert Campbell Hwy., 867/536-7469, early May–late Sept. daily 10 A.M.–6 P.M., July–Aug. daily 8 A.M.–8 P.M.) and have them put it up for you. In the center, you'll get a history lesson on the Signpost Forest, as well as the engineering feat that is the Alaska Highway through photos, displays, dioramas, and a three-projector audiovisual presentation.

Other Sights

Across from the information center, the **Northern Lights Centre** (867/536-7827, May–Sept.) is dedicated to the enthralling *aurora borealis,* also known as the northern lights. The highlight is a planetarium-type theater that shows a stunning one-hour presentation of northern lights footage shot in the Yukon. It runs several times daily from 1 P.M. to 8:30 P.M. The center also has a live feed to the Hubble telescope and a SciDome space show.

Take Eighth Street north a few blocks up from the Alaska Highway to **Wye Lake,** where a trail encircle the lake, complete with a boardwalk platform from which to view migrating

You can add your own hometown to the Signpost Forest.

THE YUKON

shorebirds and resident grebes. If you're traveling with kids, make a stop five kilometers (3.7 miles) south of town at **Lucky Lake** (June–Aug.), a day-use recreation area complete with a waterslide that will land them into the surprisingly warm lake.

Accommodations and Camping

Coming into Watson Lake from the road, you'll be tired and hungry, guaranteed. Half a dozen motels, several campgrounds, and a handful of restaurants are there to serve. **Cedar Lodge Motel** (Mile 633 Alaska Hwy., 867/536-7406, www.cedarlodge.yk.net, $85 s or d) has standard motel rooms with phones and cable TV. The hands-on owners have also developed suites in a building they moved from an abandoned mining town (from $95 s or d). Also in town is the more modern **Big Horn Hotel** (Mile 633 Alaska Hwy., 867/536-2020) with attractively appointed rooms, including kitchen suites, starting at $125 s or d.

Nugget City (867/536-2307 or 888/536-2307, www.nuggetcity.com, May–Oct.) is a large tourist complex 20 kilometers (12 miles) west of Watson Lake (just past the Cassiar turn-off). The least expensive wooden cabins ($125–210 s or d) are spotlessly clean and come with a deck and satellite TV. Even taking into consideration the nondescript interiors, they are a good value. Fancier suites come with jetted tubs and covered decks. Tent sites are $22 and large pull-through hookup sites come with power, water, and satellite TV hookups for $38–50. The on-site restaurant has a good selection of Northern foods and a nice deck.

Other camping options are **Downtown RV Park** (right in the middle of town, 867/536-2646, $32–32) with full hookups and showers, and **Watson Lake Public Campground,** which is three kilometers (1.9 miles) off the highway at Kilometer 1,025 and has no services for $17 per night.

Food

Both the **Belvedere** (867/536-7712) and **Watson Lake Hotels** (867/536-7781) have coffee shops and dining rooms open from 6 A.M.

Both also have bars, the latter decorated with Northern memorabilia.

Wolf it Down Restaurant (Nugget City, 20 km/12 mi west of town, 867/536-2307, May–Oct. daily 6:30 A.M.–9:30 P.M.) is a touristy place with decent food, including Northern specialties like bison burgers, and an in-house bakery.

WATSON LAKE TO WHITEHORSE

It's 454 kilometers (282 miles) from Watson Lake to Whitehorse. A pullout at Kilometer 1,163 marks the **Continental Divide** between rivers that drain (via the Mackenzie system) into the Arctic Ocean and those that empty (via the Yukon) into the Pacific.

◖ Dawson Peaks Resort & RV Park (Km 1,232, 867/390-2244 or 866/402-2244, www.dawsonpeaks.ca, mid-May–mid-Sept.) stands out above other lodges between Watson Lake and Teslin for both location and services. Right on Teslin Lake, it features treed tent sites ($14), RV sites ($16–27), motel rooms ($79 s or d), and basic lakeside cabins ($104–109 s or d). The restaurant not only has good food (entrées $12–19, delicious rhubarb pie $4 per slice), it has table settings on a wonderful deck overlooking the lake. Owners David Hett and Carolyn Allen will make you feel welcome, tempting you to make your stop more than a simple overnight stay with canoe rentals ($24 for a half-day) and motorboat rentals ($35 per hour); guided fishing for trout, pike, and inconnu ($75 per hour); and land and river tours (from $60 per hour).

Teslin

Just over halfway between Watson Lake and Whitehorse, Teslin (Km 1,293) is reached after crossing the impressive Nisutlin Bay Bridge (longest on the Alaska Hwy.). Its mostly Tlingit population live a traditional lifestyle: hunting, fishing, trapping, carving, and sewing. The **George Johnston Museum** (867/390-2550, daily 9 A.M.–7 P.M. in summer, $3) has displays on native culture, Yukon frontier artifacts, and one-of-a-kind photographs taken 1910–1940 by Johnston, a Tlingit hunter and trapper.

Teslin has the aforementioned **Dawson Peaks Resort & RV Park,** as well as the in-town **Yukon Motel** (867/390-2443, www.yukonmotel.com, motel rooms $85 s, $95 d, camping $27), which is on the lake and has boat rentals, gas, a restaurant, and a room filled with wildlife dioramas. Another camping option is **Teslin Lake Campground** ($14), through town at Kilometer 1,307.

Teslin to Whitehorse

It's 183 kilometers (114 miles) between Teslin and Whitehorse with the Alaska Highway closely paralleling Teslin Lake for the first 40 kilometers (25 miles) or so. At the lake's northern outlet is **Johnson's Crossing** (Km 1,346, 867/390-2607, May–Sept., campsites $22–32), which has the usual Alaska Highway set-up—campground (some sites with electricity), gas, groceries, a restaurant (delicious cinnamon buns), and showers.

At Kilometer 1,413, halfway between Jake's Corner and Whitehorse, is **[Inn on the Lake** (867/660-5253, www.exceptionalplaces.com, $229–249 s or d), the most upscale lodging along the entire Alaska Highway. The main lodge is a peeled-log building with a living room, library, solarium, and spiffy dining room with a vaulted ceiling. Each of 15 guest rooms and cottages is decorated with stylish furnishings and has a comfortable bed, quality linens, wireless Internet, and a well-appointed bathroom. Rates include breakfast and the use of canoes and kayaks.

ATLIN

The small community of Atlin lies 100 kilometers (62 miles) south of Jake's Corner, back over the border in British Columbia. It is British Columbia's northernmost and westernmost settlement. Although isolated from the rest of British Columbia, it is one of the province's most picturesque communities. The glaciated peaks of the Coast Mountains form a stunning backdrop for the town, which is on a gently sloping hill overlooking beautiful 140-kilometer-long (85-mile-long) **Atlin Lake.**

Atlin was a boomtown with more than 8,000 people during the 1898 Klondike gold rush, when gold was discovered in nearby Pine Creek. Today they're still finding some color hereabouts, but the town's population has dwindled to about 400.

The highlight of Atlin is the surrounding scenery. Wandering along the lakeshore you'll have outrageous views of sparkling peaks, glaciers, waterfalls, and mountain streams. Tied up on the lake in front of town is the **SS *Tarahne*,** a 1916 steamer that has been restored.

Sights

Atlin Historical Museum (3rd St. and Trainor St., 250/651-7522, June–early Sept. daily 9 A.M.–5:50 P.M., adult $3), housed in a 1902 schoolhouse, lets you relive the excitement of the gold rush. Scattered through town are many historic buildings and artifacts pretty much untouched from the gold-rush era.

South of Atlin along Warm Springs Road are various lakes, camping areas, and, at the end of the road, **warm springs.** The springs bubble out of the ground at a pleasant 29°C (84°F) into shallow pools surrounded by flower-filled meadows.

Practicalities

Holding a prime downtown, lakefront location is the **Atlin Inn** (1st St., 250/651-7546 or 800/682-8546, from $135 s or d) which comprises 18 motel rooms and a string of kitchen-equipped cottages. It also has a restaurant open daily at 7 A.M. and a lounge with a great patio.

For primitive camping, the first of four spots through Atlin to the south is **Pine Creek Campground** ($8), with pit toilets and firewood (no drinking water).

CARCROSS AND VICINITY

Rather than drive straight through to Whitehorse, many travelers hang a left at Jake's Corner to Carcross (a contraction of "caribou crossing"), on Highway 2 between Skagway (Alaska) and Whitehorse. This picturesque village of 400 sits at the north end of Lake Bennett, which forms the headwaters of the Yukon River. It was an important stopping point for miners during the Klondike gold rush and today is chock-a-block with buildings from that era.

Sights

Make your first stop the **Carcross Visitor Information Centre** (867/821-4431, early May–late Sept. daily 10 A.M.–6 P.M., July–Aug. daily 8 A.M.–8 P.M.), housed in a railway station that served passengers along the White Pass & Yukon Route (WP&YR). It contains not only brochures from all over the Yukon, but also fine historical exhibits. WP&YR trains crossed the original "swing bridge" in town, built to allow the riverboats to pass; walk across the bridge for a look back. A footbridge is just north of this. In the old Carcross **cemetery,** two kilometers (1.2 miles) away, rest such stampede-starting notables as Skookum Jim, Tagish Charlie, and Kate Carmack.

Accommodations and Food

The standout lodging is on Spirit Lake, a 10-minute drive north of Carcross toward Whitehorse. At **Spirit Lake Wilderness Resort** (867/821-4337 or 866/739-8566, www.spiritlakeyukon.com) the lakeside cabins ($75 s or d) are my pick for the views and rustic charm, although they don't have electricity or running water (shared shower facilities). Other choices are cottages ($65 s or d) and motel rooms ($99 s or d) that lack the atmosphere but are more comfortable. Tent sites are $25 and hookups $30–35. Activities include canoeing and horseback riding and there's an on-site restaurant.

◖ **Wheaton River Wilderness Retreat** (867/668-2997, www.wheatonriver.net, $125 s or d) is truly in the wilderness, 22 kilometers (13.7 miles) along Annie Lake Road, which branches off Highway 2 north of Spirit Lake. Accommodation is offered for up to four people in a riverfront cabin constructed with timber milled onsite by the owners. The interior is spacious, airy, and modern, with wooden furniture carved by the owners. Breakfast is $10 per person, and other meals are also available; or you can cook up a feast yourself on the wood stove or barbecue.

Whitehorse

Whitehorse is a friendly oasis in the heart of an unforgiving land. With 25,000 residents, Whitehorse is the largest city in northern Canada and is home to almost 75 percent of the Yukon's total population. It squats on the western bank of the Yukon, hemmed in by high bluffs that create something of a wind tunnel along the river. To the east, the bare rounded hulk of Grey Mountain (1,494 m/4,900 ft) fills the horizon. Whitehorse has its share of gold-rush history and nostalgia, but is not dominated by it; as the capital of Yukon Territory for the past half-century, this small city has a brash, modern frontier energy all its own. It's easy to slip into Whitehorse's strong stream of hustle and bustle, which seems to keep pace with the powerful Yukon itself. Yet the town also has a warm, homespun vitality to it, like huddling around the fire on a cold Northern night.

History

The name Whitehorse was given to the treacherous rapids encountered by stampeders, who likened them to the flowing manes of Appaloosas. An entry in an early edition of the *Klondike Nugget* described the scene:

> *Many men who ran these dangerous waters had never handled a boat in their lives until they stopped at Lake Bennett to figure out which end of their oar went into the water.... The boats filed into that tremendous first section of the canyon, dodged the whirlpool in the middle, rushed down the second section of the canyon, tossed*

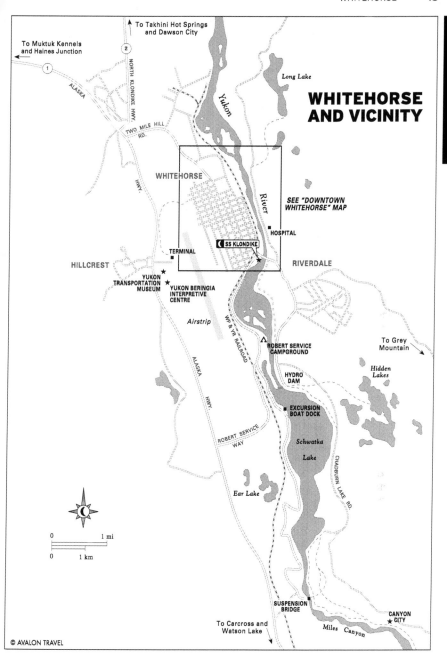

WHITEHORSE AND VICINITY

To Takhini Hot Springs and Dawson City

To Muktuk Kennels and Haines Junction

ALASKA HWY 1

NORTH KLONDIKE HWY

TWO MILE HILL RD.

Long Lake

Yukon River

WHITEHORSE

SEE "DOWNTOWN WHITEHORSE" MAP

HOSPITAL

SS KLONDIKE

TERMINAL

RIVERDALE

HILLCREST

YUKON TRANSPORTATION MUSEUM

YUKON BERINGIA INTERPRETIVE CENTRE

Airstrip

WP & YR RAILROAD

ALASKA HWY

ROBERT SERVICE CAMPGROUND

To Grey Mountain

Hidden Lakes

HYDRO DAM

EXCURSION BOAT DOCK

Schwatka Lake

ROBERT SERVICE WAY

CHADBURN LAKE RD.

Ear Lake

0   1 mi

0   1 km

SUSPENSION BRIDGE

CANYON CITY

To Carcross and Watson Lake

Miles Canyon

© AVALON TRAVEL

around for a while in the seething water of the rapids, made that stupendous turn into White Horse, as with rapidly accelerating speed they plunged into the final chaos of angry water ...

A few men drowned; many managed to hang onto their lives but lost their boats and grub-stakes. Regulations were put in place that allowed only expert handlers to pilot the rapids. Undoubtedly, this saved countless lives and supplies in the more than 7,000 boats that passed through in the first, crazy rush to the Klondike. Soon after, an eight-kilometer (five-mile) horse-drawn tramway was built around the rapids to the present site of Whitehorse, where goods were reloaded into boats to complete the journey to Dawson City. A tent city sprang up at the tramway's lower end, and Whitehorse was born.

The town's role as a transportation hub began in 1900, when the WP&YR reached Whitehorse, finally connecting Skagway (Alaska) to the Yukon. At Whitehorse, passengers and freight transferred to riverboats for the trip down the Yukon River to Dawson City. In 1942–1943 this role grew substantially, as did Whitehorse along with it, during the construction of the Alaska Highway. In 1953, Whitehorse eclipsed declining Dawson in population and importance and became the territorial seat of government. Whitehorse today thrives on highway traffic, territorial administrative duties, and its function as a supply center for Yukon mines.

SIGHTS

In addition to providing big city comforts before folks head into the wilderness, Whitehorse has enough attractions to keep you busy for at least two full days. Many of these are within walking distance of downtown and most accommodations. One natural attraction that is well worth extra time is the Yukon River. An ongoing rejuvenation program is beautifying the riverfront along downtown, with **Shipyards Park,** at the north end of downtown, a sign of what will come in the future.

Shipyards features a wide-open green space, picnic tables, viewing platform, and stage.

◖ SS *Klondike*

Start your visit to Whitehorse with a tour of this National Historic Site—the largest stern-wheeler ever to ply the waters of the Yukon, the SS *Klondike,* which is dry-docked along 2nd Avenue at the south end of town (867/667-3910, mid-May–mid-Sept. daily 9:30 A.M.–5 P.M., $6.05 per person for the tour). Launched in 1929 and rebuilt after it sank in 1936, the *Klondike* made 15 round-trips a season, requiring one and a half days and 40 cords of wood for the downstream trip to Dawson, four and a half days and 120 cords back to Whitehorse. The *Klondike* is beautifully and authentically restored, right down to the 1937 *Life* magazines and the food stains on the waiters' white coats. Bridges erected along the road to Dawson in the mid-1950s blocked the steamer's passage and she has sat in the same spot since her last run in 1955. The best way to learn about the vessel and her colorful history is by joining a tour that runs every 30 minutes, proceeding from the boiler, freight, and engine deck, up to the dining room and first-class cabins, and finally up to the bridge.

MacBride Museum

North of the visitors center and across the road from the river is the excellent MacBride Museum (1124 1st Ave. at Wood St., 867/667-2709, summer daily 9:30 A.M.–5:30 P.M., the rest of the year Tues.–Sat. noon–4 P.M., adult $8, senior $7, child $4.50). The main building is a sod-roofed log cabin filled with historical items, including stuffed Yukon wildlife and hundreds of gold-rush photographs. Surrounding it are other buildings and equipment: the old government telegraph office, engine No. 51 from the WP&YR, Sam McGee's cabin, and even a one-ton copper nugget.

Yukon Beringia Interpretive Centre

Named for the landmass that once linked Asia

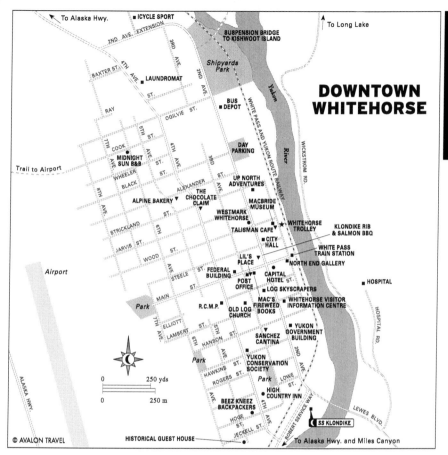

DOWNTOWN WHITEHORSE

© AVALON TRAVEL

and North America, this dramatic multimedia center (Alaska Hwy., 867/667-8855 May–Sept. daily 9 A.M.–6 P.M., the rest of the year Sun. 1–5 P.M., adult $7.50, senior $6.50, child $5) out by the airport contains life-size exhibits of animals from the last Ice Age, including a spectacular 12,000-year-old, four-meter-tall (12-foot) woolly mammoth skeleton. Visitors will learn about the prehistoric animals that once roamed the north through exhibits, computer kiosks, dioramas, and a fascinating 30-minute film. A reconstruction of a 24,000-year-old archaeological site is also here, plus a gift shop and café.

Yukon Transportation Museum

Located next to the Beringia Interpretive Centre, this is one of the finest museums in the north (30 Electra Cres., 867/668-4792, mid-May–Aug. daily 10 A.M.–6 P.M., adult $6, senior $5, child $3). You could easily spend a few hours examining the many excellent displays and watching the long historical videos. Here's just a sample: Look up to view *Queen of the Yukon,* the first commercial aircraft in the territory, hanging from the ceiling; take the Golden Stairs up to the second floor, where murals and artifacts re-create the gold rush from Skagway to Dawson; sit in Lake Annie, a WP&YR railcar, and watch the 30-minute video while the model train circles the track; and check out the Alcan room with a fascinating video on the highway's construction. Out front is a DC-3 that acts as the world's largest weathervane.

Schwatka Lake and Miles Canyon

Cross the bridge beside the *Klondike* and take Lewis Boulevard south or walk along the riverside trail south 4.5 kilometers (2.8 miles) toward the **Whitehorse Dam** that created Schwatka Lake, tamed the once-feared White Horse Rapids, and now provides electricity for the city. The world's longest wooden **fishway** (366 m/1,200 ft) allows fish to get around the dam and up to their spawning grounds upriver. Three underwater windows inside the fishway building (867/633-5965, June–early Sept. daily 8:30 A.M.–8:30 P.M.) give you a good look at the chinook (king) salmon (late July–early Sept. is best).

From the dam, continue south on Chadburn Lake Road to the head of the lake where the Yukon River flows through spectacular Miles Canyon. A path along the canyon leads to the distinctive **Lowe Suspension Bridge** (1923), the first bridge across the Yukon—the views are superb.

Continue two kilometers (1.2 miles) beyond the bridge, staying on the east side, to reach the site of **Canyon City,** which slipped into oblivion after the opening of the railway in 1900 put an end to river travel above Whitehorse.

As an alternative to accessing these sights by road, consider walking. It's 10 kilometers (6.2 miles) round-trip from downtown, with the option of crossing the suspension bridge and returning along the west bank of the river, or jumping aboard a city transit bus (hourly along South Access Rd.) to get back to town. Another way to see the lake and surrounding sights is with **Yukon River Cruises** (867/668-4716, adult $30, child $15) aboard the MV *Schwatka*, a tour boat that departs daily at 2 P.M. June–early September (plus 6 P.M. in mid-July to mid-Aug.) for two-hour cruises. The departure point is along Miles Canyon Road one

kilometer (0.6 miles) south of downtown on the *west* side of the dam.

Takhini Hot Springs

These odorless (no sulfur) hot springs (867/456-8000, mid-May–mid-June daily noon–10 P.M., mid-June–mid-Sept. daily 8 A.M.–10 P.M.) bubble out of the ground at 36°C (96°F) north of Whitehorse. They have been developed and are as popular with locals as they are with visitors. All-day access is adult $8, senior $6.50, child $5.75. The attached café has some of the best chicken soup north of Vancouver. The hot springs campground costs $16.50 for tents and $25–35 for RVs and trailers (this is a good place to spend the night, take an early dip, then hit the road to Dawson). Get to Takhini by driving 18 kilometers (11.2 miles) north from Whitehorse toward Dawson City, then take the 10-kilometer (6.2-mile) side road to the west (it's well signposted).

RECREATION
Historical and Nature Walks

Whitehorse is small enough that you can cover downtown by foot. A pleasant paved **walkway** follows the Yukon River from the SS *Klondike* to the north end of town.

To learn more about local history, take a volunteer-led 45-minute historical walking tour (June–Aug. Mon.–Sat. at 9 A.M., 11 A.M., 1 P.M., and 3 P.M.) of downtown Whitehorse buildings offered by the **Yukon Historical & Museums Association.** It leaves from Donnenworth House (3126 3rd Ave., 867/667-4704). If the tour times don't fit into your plans, stop by the Donnenworth House, pick up the walking tour book, and take a self-guided tour.

The **Yukon Conservation Society** (302 Hawkins St., 867/668-5678, Mon.–Fri. 10 A.M.–4 P.M.) leads a variety of hikes, from two to six hours, several times a day in July and early August. One of the most interesting is a two-hour trip to Miles Canyon; or if the family is with you, the kids may enjoy joining the association's Kid Ed-Ventures program for a morning. The hikes are free; bring bug spray,

FLOATING THE YUKON

Every year hardy souls re-create the 742-kilometer (464-mile) route taken by stampeders heading to the Klondike goldfields by floating the Yukon River from Whitehorse. The most authentic way to travel is by canoe, which takes 12–15 days. While this is a trip for experienced wilderness travelers only, two Whitehorse companies make organization easy by providing rentals and transfers. Both companies also offer the option of floating the river as part of a guided tour.

Kanoe People (867/668-4899, www.kanoepeople.com) has been around the longest (since 1974), and rents canoes for $30 per day or $180 per week. They specialize in one-way rentals to Carmacks or Dawson and guided tours, such as a seven-day river trip with meals and accommodations for $2,000. **Up North Adventures** (103 Strickland St., 867/667-7035, www.upnorth.yk.ca) also offers canoe rentals (as well as bike and kayak rentals) with a local drop-off and pick-up service perfect for a single day on the river. For example, pay $65 per person for a full-day rental and return transportation from Lake Laberge. Their 17-day Whitehorse to Dawson float is $2,280 per person.

wear sturdy boots, and have a lunch for the longer excursions. You can also buy self-guided trail booklets at the society's office and set out on your own.

◖ Dog-Mushing

Also known as dog-sledding, sled-dogging, or simply mushing, what was once a form of transportation has grown into a major winter pastime, both as a recreational activity and as a competitive sport. One of the legends of the mushing world is Frank Turner, who owns and operates **Muktuk Kennels** (west of Whitehorse toward Haines Jct., 867/668-3647, www.muktuk.com), which is a place of work for Turner and his team of handlers, but also a bona fide

tourist attraction. Through summer, visitors are invited to take a look around for $15, but much more informative is the three-hour tour of the kennels daily at 1 P.M. for $35, or $75 with a dinner of Northern delicacies. In fall (Sept.–Nov.), you can join a training run with the dogs aboard an ATV ($85). As you'd expect, it is in winter that the action really cranks up, with options that range from a full-day mushing trip ($185–265 pp) to attending a weeklong Rookie Ranch ($2,270).

Biking and Golf

Whitehorse is relatively flat, making biking easy and fun. Rent mountain bikes from **Up North Adventures** (103 Strickland St., 867/667-7035). If you're interested in joining up with some locals, drop by **Icycle Sport** (9002 Quartz Rd., 867/668-7559) and ask about evening group rides after the shop closes at 6 P.M.

Along the Alaska Highway south of the city is **Meadow Lakes Golf Resort** (867/668-4653), a short nine-hole course kept in excellent condition through the summer golfing season. As with the course in Yellowknife, one of the unique features is tee times as late as 10:30 P.M. in late June and early July.

SHOPPING

A number of fine galleries are scattered around town. The Northern Fibres Guild produces a free booklet that describes local artists with illustrations of their work; it's available at the Visitor Information Centre. Well worth a visit are the **North End Gallery** (118 1st Ave., 867/393-3590) and the **Midnight Sun Gallery** (205 Main St., 867/668-4350), the latter featuring the brightly colored, Northern-themed paintings of Ted Harrison.

Across from the information center, **Folknits** (3123 3rd Ave., 867/456-4192) sells spinning fiber and finished knitwear made from *quviuq,* the fine underhair of the musk ox. Look for the log cabin with two moose on the roof.

Bookstores
Mac's Fireweed Books (203 Main St.,

867/668-6104, www.yukonbooks.com) is the biggest and most complete bookstore in the Yukon, with a large selection of local- and general-interest books, children's books, and magazines. It's open daily until midnight in the summer. If you can't find what you're looking for using the in-store searchable database at **Well-Read Books** (4137 4th Ave., 867/393-2987, www.wellreadbooks.yk.net), the knowledgeable staff will lead you in the right direction when it comes to looking through their used book collection.

ENTERTAINMENT AND EVENTS

Frantic Follies is one of many vaudeville revues along the route north to Alaska that is styled on the stage shows that entertained stampeders back in the days of the Klondike gold rush. The Follies are performed nightly at the Westmark Whitehorse (201 Wood St., 867/668-2042, May–mid-Sept. nightly at 8:30 P.M., adult $24, child $10).

Whitehorse has no lack of rowdy bars and none are as popular as **"The Cap"** (in the Capital Hotel, 103 Main St., 867/667-2565)— although renovated it's still music central for Whitehorse, with rock bands seven nights a week. **Yukon Brewing Company** (102 Copper Rd., 867/668-4183) is the only brewery in the territory. Free tours (with samples) are offered daily at 2 P.M. and a gift shop is open daily 11 A.M.–6 P.M. These brews are available throughout Canada, but they are also available on tap throughout Whitehorse.

Festivals and Events

One of the Yukon's biggest events is the **Yukon Quest** (867/668-4711, www.yukonquest.com) a 1,600-kilometer (1,000-mile) dog-mushing race between Whitehorse and Fairbanks held each February. As the race is winding down, Whitehorse spins into action with the **Frostbite Music Festival** (www.frostbitefest.ca), featuring an eclectic mix of concerts, dances, and workshops highlighting Canada's thriving independent music industry.

The summer solstice (June 21) is celebrated with a **Midnight Sun Golf Tournament** at Mountainview Golf Course (867/633-6020). The **Yukon International Storytelling Festival** (www.storytelling.yk.net) attracts storytellers from around the world who combine their words with music and dance. The venue is the **Yukon Arts Centre** (300 College Dr., 867/667-8574), which hosts events year-round.

ACCOMMODATIONS AND CAMPING

Whitehorse has a surprising number of motels and hotels for its size: 23, accounting for more than 900 rooms. The competition, of course, works to the traveler's advantage, and some of the digs are actually affordable.

Under $50

Beez Kneez Bakpakers (408 Hoge St., 867/456-2333, www.bzkneez.com, dorm $25, $60 s or d) has dorm beds, private rooms with two single beds, and a cabin that sleeps two. Other amenities include a living room, a communal kitchen, laundry facilities, free use of bikes, and Internet access.

$50-100

[**Historical Guest House** (5128 5th Ave., 867/668-3907, www.yukongold.com, $85–110 s, $95–110 d) is a comfortable downtown home that was built in 1907 and has been extensively restored, exposing much of the original hand-hewn log work. Each of the two upstairs guest rooms has its own bathroom, while the basement holds a self-contained suite. Other amenities include a communal kitchen and living area, and out back is a garden and barbecue. Rates include a light, self-serve breakfast. The owners live next door.

If you're planning on traveling as far north as Whitehorse, you're more adventurous than most travelers, so why not do something really unique and stay on a ranch with 100 mushing dogs? You can at **Muktuk Adventures** (west of Whitehorse toward Haines Jct., 867/668-3647, www.muktuk.com, $85–95 s or d including breakfast), on the property of mushing legend

Frank Turner. Accommodation choices are wooden cabins or a room in the main lodge. Dinner is provided at an extra charge. The property is right on the Takhini River and in addition to tours of the facility, there are canoe rentals, hiking, and trail riding.

$100-150

For modern, comfortable bed-and-breakfast accommodations within walking distance of downtown restaurants and shops, make reservations at **Midnight Sun B&B** (6188 6th Ave., 867/667-2255 or 866/284-4448, www.midnightsunbb.com, $119 s, $135–140 d). Four of the five guest rooms are en suite, and one has a private bathroom down the hall. Each room also has a TV, phone, and Internet access. Guests have use of a lounge and kitchen.

Sundog Retreat (off the Klondike Hwy., 867/633-4183, www.sundogretreat.com, $130–200 per cabin) comprises six cabins spread over 60 hectares (160 acres) on a lightly treed property north of downtown (see the website for a map). Each cabin has a kitchen and one or two bedrooms; some have decks and all are very private.

$150-200

My choice for downtown hotel accommodation is the **High Country Inn** (4051 4th Ave., 867/667-4471 or 800/554-4471, www.highcountryinn.yk.ca, $169–259 s or d), a large and well-appointed hostelry with a variety of accommodations, starting at $169 s or d for standard rooms, and going all the way up to $269 for the Presidential Suite. The hotel has a fitness room, a business center with Internet access, and its own airport shuttle. Downstairs is a bistro-style restaurant and a lounge with a large patio.

Camping

The prime choice for tenters (no RVs allowed) is █ **Robert Service Campground** (South Access Rd., 867/668-3721, www.robertservicecampground.com, mid-May–Sept., $18), a two-kilometer (1.2-mile) drive or 20-minute walk south of town along the Millennium

Trail. It has a small store and café, showers, and free firewood. Government-run **Wolf Creek Campground** ($14), 11 kilometers (6.8 miles) south of Whitehorse along the Alaska Highway, has campsites for tents and RVs (but no hookups), a nature trail, water, outhouses, and cooking shelters.

Near the south entrance to town, **Hi Country RV Park** (91357 Alaska Hwy., 867/667-7445 or 877/458-3806, www.hicountryrvyukon.com, tents $16, hookups $25–33) is one of a half-dozen private campgrounds spread along the Alaska Highway within a five-minute drive of downtown. It has 130 sites spread among the trees, modern shower facilities, a laundry, RV wash, dump station, wireless Internet, and convenience store. Farther south, **Pioneer RV Park** (91091 Alaska Hwy., 867/668-5944, www.pioneer-rv-park.com, May–Sept., tents $15, hookups $22–28) has a similar setting as well as an on-site mechanic, discounted fuel for guests, and wireless Internet access.

FOOD
Cafes and Other Cheap Eats

Even though chains such as Starbucks have made an appearance in Whitehorse, go beyond what you know and search out **Midnight Sun Coffee Roaster** (9002 Quartz Rd., 867/668-7559, Mon.–Sat. 8 A.M.–5 P.M.), with coffee that is as good as you'll find anywhere. It comes with locally inspired monikers like Sam McGee's Black. Also well worth a visit is **The Chocolate Claim** (305 Strickland St., 867/667-2202, Mon.–Fri. 7:30 A.M.–6 P.M., Sat 8:30 A.M.–6 P.M., lunches $6.50–9), an arty space with handmade chocolates, freshly baked sunflower bread, sandwiches, savory soups, and cappuccino.

In a two-story log building just off 4th Avenue on the north side of downtown, █ **Alpine Bakery** (411 Alexander St., 867/668-6871, Mon.–Sat. 8 A.M.–6 P.M.) bakes wholesome European-style breads with organic ingredients, but they aren't cheap. A specialty is Expedition Bread, which stays edible for up to a month. The bakery is also part deli.

Lil's Place (209 Main St., 867/668-3545,

daily 7 A.M.–9 P.M., $5.50–12) is set up as a 1950s diner complete with vinyl booths, a jukebox, gumball machines, and a menu of burgers and shakes.

Canadian

Right downtown, dining at **(Bistro on Fourth** (High Country Inn, 4051 4th Ave., 867/667-4471, 7 A.M.–9:30 P.M., $15–31) combines Northern favorites with a clean, comfortable atmosphere and reasonable prices. The best choices focus on classic dishes with a Northern twist, such as a caribou burger. Most steak and seafood mains, including choices such as pork ribs barbecued on the heated deck, are under $30.

Housed in Whitehorse's oldest commercial building, the **Klondike Rib & Salmon BBQ** (2116 2nd Ave., 867/667-7554, mid-May–Sept. daily for dinner, $14–29) has a family-friendly atmosphere of long tables covered with checked tablecloths and a finger-lickin' menu. The house specialty is barbecued ribs, but you'll also find steaks, Caesar salad, smoked salmon, halibut fish-and-chips, miner's soup with caribou sausage, and bumbleberry pie. It's busy, noisy, fun, and tasty. Close by, the **Talisman Café** (River View Hotel, 102 Wood St., 867/667-7801, Mon.–Sat. 7 A.M.–8 P.M., Sun 6 A.M.–4 P.M.) is very different. The atmosphere is heady and the food runs the entire spectrum—from bannock and jam ($3) at breakfast to couscous salad ($7) and a Mediterranean platter ($18) in the evening.

Mexican

Sanchez Cantina (211 Hanson St., 867/668-5858, Mon.–Sat. 11:30 A.M.–2:30 P.M. and 5–9:30 P.M., $10–16.50) is a casual, quiet place with familiar Mexican favorites. Sides of salsa and guacamole are made in-house and are delicious.

INFORMATION

Whitehorse Visitor Information Centre (corner 2nd Ave. and Lambert St., 867/667-3084, early May–late Sept. daily 10 A.M.–6 P.M. extended to daily 8 A.M.–8 P.M. July–Aug., the rest of the year Mon.–Fri. 8:30 A.M.–5 P.M., Sat. 10 A.M.–2 P.M.) promotes both Whitehorse and the Yukon. The **City of Whitehorse** website (www.whitehorse.ca) is a handy pre-trip reference.

The excellent **Whitehorse Public Library** (2071 2nd Ave., 867/667-5239, Mon.–Fri. 10 A.M.–9 P.M., Sat. 10 A.M.–6 P.M., Sun. 1–9 P.M.) is directly across from the visitors center. It has a good selection of Northern literature, newspapers from around the world, and public Internet access.

GETTING THERE

The airport is right above town on the bluff. You can't miss the "world's largest weathervane"—the restored DC-3 (mounted on a moveable pedestal) that points its nose into the wind. From downtown, get to the airport by going north along 4th Avenue to the Alaska Highway and take a left, or go south out 2nd Avenue and turn right. Most hotels provide a shuttle, or you can catch a cab for around $14 to downtown. From its Whitehorse hub, local carrier **Air North** (800/661-0407, www.flyairnorth.com) has flights to and from the southern gateways of Edmonton, Calgary, and Vancouver, as well as onward flights to Dawson City and Inuvik. **Air Canada** (888/247-2262) has service to Whitehorse from both Vancouver and Calgary. **First Air** (800/267-1247, www.firstair.ca) has scheduled service between Whitehorse and Yellowknife (NWT) three times a week.

Whitehorse Bus Depot (2191 2nd Ave. behind Qwanlin Mall, 867/668-2223) is the northern terminus for **Greyhound.** In summer, one bus a day (departs 1 P.M.) heads south along the Alaska Highway. The only bus service that continues west from Whitehorse to Alaska is **Alaska Direct Bus Line** (867/668-4833 or 800/770-6652, www.alaskadirectbusline.com, mid-May–Sept.), to Anchorage (US$220) and Fairbanks (US$190). **Alaska/Yukon Trails** (800/770-7275, www.alaskashuttle.com) charges US$149 each way for the shuttle trip between Whitehorse and Dawson City, with onward travel to Fairbanks (Alaska) an option.

GETTING AROUND

Whitehorse Transit (867/668-7433, Mon.–Sat. 6 A.M.–7 P.M., Fri. to 10 P.M., $2.50) operates a citywide public bus service. Pick up a schedule at the visitor centre or from the drivers. All routes begin and end beside Canadian Tire, opposite Qwanlin Mall.

Local taxi companies are **5th Avenue Taxi** (867/667-4111), **Whitehorse Taxi** (867/393-6543), and **Yellow Cab** (867/668-4811).

All major car-rental companies are represented at the airport. If you're planning on renting a vehicle in Whitehorse, check mileage allowances. Unlike elsewhere in Canada, companies do not include unlimited travel.

For example, **National** charges $70 a day and $420 a week for their smallest vehicles, with a maximum of 200 free kilometers (93 miles) per day.

Whitehorse is a popular starting point for European travelers who want to explore the Yukon and Alaska in a campervan, so you'll find plenty of choices. Plan on spending around $1,200 per week for a truck and camper, or $1,800 per week for a 24-foot motor home, both with 100 kilometers (62 miles) free per day. Local rental companies include **CanaDream** (867/668-3610, www.canadream.com) and **Fraserway** (867/668-3438 or 800/806-1976, www.fraserway.com).

Whitehorse to Beaver Creek

Before leaving Whitehorse, you need to decide whether to take the Alaska Highway straight through to Alaska or continue north to Dawson City and then continue along the Top of the World Highway, which loops back down to the Alaska Highway at Tok (Alaska). The latter option adds less than 200 kilometers (120 miles) to the distance between Whitehorse and Tok, while taking in Dawson City, a must-stop on any Northern itinerary. The entire loop, beginning and ending at Whitehorse, is 1,480 kilometers (920 miles).

This section covers the direct route to Alaska, along the Alaska Highway to Beaver Creek. The total distance to the border is 460 kilometers (187 miles). Haines Junction is the only town of any consequence en route, beyond which the highway parallels Kluane National Park.

Whitehorse to Haines Junction

It's an easy 160-kilometer (100-mile) drive to Haines Junction from the capital. The scenery doesn't really become memorable until the highway closes in on Haines Junction, when the Kluane Icefield Ranges and the foothills of the St. Elias Mountains start to dominate the view; when it's clear, Mount Hubbard

(4,577 m/15,000 ft) looms high and white straight ahead.

A worthwhile stop is Kilometer 1,604, 21 kilometers (13 miles) east of Haines Junction. Here a log bridge dating to the early 1900s has been rebuilt. Walk out onto it to compare the log action with the steel-supported highway bridge.

Government campgrounds between Whitehorse and Haines Junction are located at Kilometer 1,543; Kilometer 1,602; and Kilometer 1,628.

HAINES JUNCTION

Established in 1942 as a base camp for Alaska Highway construction, this town of 800 is the largest between Whitehorse and Tok and is the gateway to Kluane National Park, the most accessible of the Yukon's three national parks. It's also the first town north of Haines (Alaska), and so sees a lot of traffic from the ferry passing through.

Sights

At the village square near the intersection of the Alaska and Haines Highways, a grotesque sculpture of mountains, mammals, and humans has been placed. Ironically, it's part of a Yukon beautification program. It looks more like a misshapen cupcake with really ugly icing. Here you can also read the signboards describing the history and attractions of the Haines Junction area and sign your name in the gigantic guest book. Just up the road toward Whitehorse is **Our Lady of the Way Church,** built in 1954 by a Catholic priest who converted an old Quonset hut by adding a wooden front, a shrine on top, and a steeple with bell in back.

Accommodations and Camping

Haines has a bunch of motels to choose from (listed in the territorial tourism guide), along with the following three choices.

Paddle Wheel Adventures (867/634-2683, www.paddlewheeladventures.com) rents modern Quonset-style huts, each with a cooking facilities and a private bathroom, for a reasonable $60 per night. Primarily outfitters, they also rent canoes and bikes and lead guided raft and fishing tours.

The Cabin (27 km/16.8 mi south of Haines Jct. on Hwy. 3, 867/634-2626, www.thecabinyukon.com, $85 s, $95 d) comprises five rustic cabins, each with a kitchenette and deck with views extending over Kluane National Park.

The **Raven Hotel** (867/634-2500, www.ravenhotelyukon.com, May–Sept., $120 s, $135 d including breakfast) offers the 12 nicest motel rooms in town, a restaurant with lots of local specialties, and an art gallery/gift shop. You can't miss it; the Raven looks like a modular mansion, right in the middle of town.

Right downtown, **Kluane RV Kampground** (867/634-2709, www.kluanerv.ca, tents $18, hookups $24–30) separates tenters from RVers but offers lots of services for both. For in-town camping, the tent sites are pleasant, with lots of trees, and barbecues and firewood supplied. The sites with hookups come with cable TV and Internet access, but don't have much privacy. Other amenities include a shower block, laundry, car and RV wash, grocery store, and gas.

Food

Village Bakery (867/634-2867, May–Sept.) is a popular hangout, with delicious muffins, strudels, doughnuts, and cheese sticks, as well as breads, sourdough sandwiches (try the smoked salmon, which is smoked on-site), soups, quiches, sourdough pizzas, lasagna, meat pies, and whatever else the good cooks feel like creating. On Friday at 6:30 P.M. there's a salmon barbecue ($17) and live music on the deck.

Several of the hotels also serve meals, including—most notably—the **Raven Hotel** (867/634-2500, May–Sept. daily 5:30–10 P.M., $18–31). The menu here changes daily, but the choices are always varied and thoughtful. Considering the remote location, the owners do a great job of sourcing fresh produce to go with lots of local game and seafood. Views of the snowcapped peaks of Kluane National Park are a bonus.

Information

Haines Junction Visitor Information Centre (867/634-2345, early May–late Sept. daily 10 A.M.–6 P.M., July–Aug. daily 8 A.M.–8 P.M.) is a provincially operated facility on the highway through town.

◖ KLUANE NATIONAL PARK

The lofty ice-capped mountains of southwest Yukon, overflowing with glaciers and flanked by lower ranges rich in wildlife, have been set aside as 21,980-square-kilometer (8,490-square-mile) Kluane (Kloo-AH-nee) National Park. Although the Alaska and Haines Highways, which run along the fringe of the park, make it accessible, Kluane is a wilderness hardly touched by human hands; once you leave the highways you'll see few other people. No roads run into the park itself, so to experience the true magnificence of this wilderness you must embark on an overnight hike or take a flightseeing trip.

The Land

The St. Elias Range, running from Alaska through the Yukon to British Columbia, is the highest mountain range in North America and the second-highest coastal range in the world (only the Andes are higher). **Mount Logan,** at 6,050 meters (19,850 feet), is the highest peak in Canada. The ranges you see from the Alaska Highway are impressive enough, but only through gaps can you glimpse the fantastic Icefield Ranges lying directly behind. These peaks are surrounded by a gigantic ice field plateau 2,500–3,000 meters (8,200–9,800 feet) high, the largest non-polar ice field in the world, occupying a little more than half the park. Radiating out from the ice field like spokes on a wheel are valley glaciers up to 60 kilometers (37 miles) long, some very active. Such is the importance of this area that—together with Wrangell–Saint Elias and Glacier Bay National Parks in Alaska, and Tatshenshini-Alsek Provincial Park in British Columbia—Kluane has been declared a World Heritage Site by UNESCO.

Although more than half of Kluane is ice, rock, and snow, the remainder includes habitat that holds large populations of wildlife. Some 4,000 Dall sheep—one of the world's largest populations—reside on the high open hillsides northwest of Kaskawulsh Glacier and elsewhere in the park. Many can be seen from the highway in the vicinity of Sheep Mountain. Kluane also has significant numbers of moose, caribou, mountain goats, and grizzly bears.

Flightseeing

Flightseeing over the park is available from the Haines Junction Airport. The one-hour flight affords a spectacular view of Mount Logan plus several glaciers and is highly recommended if you happen to be there on a clear day. Contact **Sifton Air** (867/634-2916). Prices with **Trans North Helicopters** (867/634-2242) start at $180 per person for a 30-minute glacier tour. Trans North is based beyond Haines Junction around Kilometer 1,698.

Tours

If you're not comfortable exploring the backcountry without a local guide, consider using **Kluane Ecotours** (867/634-2600, www.kluaneco.com), which offers day and overnight trips on foot and in kayaks and canoes, including a paddling/hiking combo to King's Throne.

Practicalities

Easily accessible 27 kilometers (17 miles) south of Haines Junction and within Kluane National Park is **Kathleen Lake Campground** (867/634-7250, mid-May–mid-Sept., $16), with 39 sites between the highway and the lake. Amenities are limited to firewood ($9 for a fire permit), drinking water, and pit toilets, but it's a delightful spot that is a popular launching spot for kayaks and canoes. It also has a short interpretive trail and is the starting point for a five-kilometer (3.1-mile) trek up to the King's Throne, so named for its sweeping views across the park; allow five hours round-trip.

In Haines Junction, the **Kluane Visitor Reception Centre** (867/634-2293, www.pc.gc.ca, mid-May–mid-Sept. daily 9 A.M.–5 P.M.) has a relief map of the park and an excellent 20-minute sight-and-sound slide show presented every half hour. On the Alaska Highway 72 kilometers (45 miles) north of Haines Junction, **Tachal Dhal Visitor Centre** (867/734-7250, mid-May–mid-Sept. daily 9 A.M.–4 P.M.) has a spotting scope to look for Dall sheep on nearby Sheep Mountain (late Aug.–mid June is the best time of year for sheep-spotting).

HAINES JUNCTION TO BEAVER CREEK

For most of the 300 kilometers (186 miles) to Beaver Creek, the Alaska Highway parallels Kluane National Park or Kluane Wildlife Sanctuary—a comparatively well-populated, civilized, and stunningly scenic stretch of the road. Along the way are three government campgrounds (Km 1,725; Km 1,853; and Km 1,913), three little settlements, and a dozen lodges.

At **Soldier's Summit,** one kilometer (0.6 miles) north of the Tachal Dhal Visitor Information Centre, a sign commemorates the official opening of the Alcan on November 20, 1942, a mere eight months after construction began; an interpretive trail from the parking area leads up to the site of the dedication ceremony.

Destruction Bay

This tiny town at Kilometer 1,743 was named when the original road-construction camp was destroyed by a windstorm in 1942. Destruction Bay has a gas station, the 32-room **Talbot Arm Motel** (867/841-4461, $90 s, $105 d), a cafeteria and dining room, an RV park, showers, general store, and gift shop.

Burwash Landing

On Kluane Lake, 127 kilometers (79 miles) northwest of Haines Junction, is Burwash Landing, population 90. The fine **Kluane Museum of Natural History** (867/841-5561, mid-May–mid-Sept. daily 9 A.M.–6:30 P.M., adult $5, child $4) includes a wildlife exhibit, native artifacts, a large model of the area, a theater where a wildlife video is shown, and some interesting fossils. Also take a gander at **Our Lady of the Rosary Church,** a log structure built in 1944.

Burwash Landing Resort (867/841-4441) has hotel rooms from $95 s or d, a restaurant, lounge, RV park, and boat rentals. The cafeteria is huge, there's a fine dining room, and the bar gets raucous most nights—check out the back wallpapered with money. You can boat and fish in the lake from here; guides are available.

BEAVER CREEK

The last place with facilities in the Yukon, Beaver Creek is a tiny town (population 110) with a big travel-based economy.

Accommodations and Food

On the west side of town, the **1202 Motor Inn** (867/862-7600 or 800/764-7601 in Alaska or 800/661-0540 in western Canada, www.1202motorinn.ca, $85–175 s or d, RV sites $28) has motel rooms in an older wing, more modern units, large kitchen-equipped suites, and parking for RVs. The complex also has a rustic log dining room, a lounge, public Internet access, and gas (which will be cheaper on the U.S. side of the border). It's also open year-round. The biggest place in town is the **Westmark Inn Beaver Creek** (867/862-7501 or 800/544-0970, www.westmarkhotels.com, mid-May–mid-Sept., $99 s or d), with 174 tiny, nondescript rooms aimed at the escorted-tour crowd.

The Westmark hosts performances of **Rendezvous Dinner Theatre,** a lighthearted musical theatre nightly in the summer. It costs $55 for dinner and the show or $25 for the show alone.

Information

Beaver Creek Visitor Information Centre (867/862-7321, early May–late Sept. daily 10 A.M.–6 P.M., July–Aug. daily 8 A.M.–8 P.M.) is operated by the Yukon government as an information resource for travelers entering the territory from Alaska.

Onward to Alaska

The Canada–U.S. border is 32 kilometers (20 miles) west of Beaver Creek and the **U.S. Customs post** is another one kilometer (0.6 miles) west. Heading into Alaska, be sure to turn your watches back one hour to Alaska Standard Time. Traveling in the opposite direction, **Canadian Customs** is well inside Canada, just three kilometers (1.9 miles) northwest of Beaver Creek. Both posts are open 24 hours a day year-round, and you'll need a passport regardless of your citizenship or which direction you're headed.

If you're reading this before leaving home, begin planning your Alaska travels by contacting the **Alaska Travel Industry Association** (907/465-2017, www.travelalaska.com) and requesting an information package. The best guidebook out there is Don Pitcher's *Moon Alaska* (Avalon Travel Publishing). In Whitehorse, you'll find copies at Mac's Fireweed Books.

Whitehorse to Dawson City

It's 536 kilometers (333 miles) north from Whitehorse to Dawson City. Allow six or seven hours non-stop, or stretch the trip out to a full day or two by stopping at the places detailed below.

Lake Laberge

Lake Laberge, 62 kilometers (38.5 miles) from Whitehorse, is famous primarily as the site of the burning of the corpse in Robert Service's immortal poem "Cremation of Sam McGee." The excellent trout fishing here has also been well-known since stampeder days, when the fish were barged to Dawson by the ton. You can also continue 22 kilometers (14 miles) north to **Fox Lake Campground,** with summertime swimming.

Carmacks

A little more than 180 kilometers (120 miles) from Whitehorse, the river town of Carmacks (population 420) is named for George Washington Carmack, credited with the Bonanza Creek strike that triggered the famous Klondike gold rush.

Get the lay of town by driving down Three Gold Road (at the Carmacks Hotel) to the Yukon River. A two-kilometer (1.2 miles) **boardwalk** runs along the river from here to a park, complete with a gazebo. There are benches, viewing platforms, and interpretive signs along the way. **Tage Cho Hudan Interpretive Centre** (867/863-5830) exhibits archaeological displays and a diorama of a mammoth snare, plus interpretive trails and a gift shop. Find it at the second driveway north of the bridge.

Hotel Carmacks (867/863-5221, www.hotelcarmacks.com, from $95 s or d) rents modern rooms and cabins in a building behind the main complex. Here you'll find a large lounge sporting a couple of pool tables and an interesting brass railing along the bar, perfect for bellying up to. Part of its restaurant occupies the old Carmacks roadhouse, built in 1903 and the only remaining roadhouse of the 16 that once operated between Whitehorse and Dawson.

Five Finger Rapids

North of Carmacks 25 kilometers (15.5 miles) is a pullout overlooking Five Finger Rapids, where four rock towers here choke the river, dividing it into five channels through which the current rips. At **Five Finger Rapids Recreation Site** a wooden platform overlooks the river, and stairs lead down to the river. Allow an hour or so for the round-trip to the river—a nice little walk to break up the drive.

Pelly Crossing

In another 108 kilometers (67 miles) you come to Pelly Crossing, roughly halfway between Whitehorse and Dawson. Downtown, interpretive panels describe the town and its native population, who moved upstream from remote Fort Selkirk after the Klondike Highway was completed in the 1950s.

Silver Trail

The first settlement north of Pelly River is **Stewart Crossing,** the site of an 1883 trading post and the last gas stop before Dawson City, another 181 kilometers (112 miles) north.

At this point, the Silver Trail (Hwy. 11) branches northeast through a heavily mined area of silver deposits. Two small towns and loads of history make a detour worthwhile.

Mayo (population 400), above a wide bend of the Stewart River, was once a bustling silver-mining center, with the ore transported out of the wilderness by stern-wheeler, eventually reaching smelters in San Francisco. Stop by the two-story **Binet House** (304 Second Ave., 867/996-2926, May–Sept. daily 10 A.M.–6 P.M.) for a rundown of the Mayo District, including historical photos; displays on the geology, minerals, flora, and fauna of the area; and silver samples. The **Bedrock Motel** (north side of town, 867/996-2290, www.

bedrockmotel.com, $95 s or d) is a modern wooden lodge with 12 clean, comfortable guest rooms, as well as RV parking ($25). Amenities include a laundry and canoe rentals.

From Mayo, it's eight kilometers (five miles) of paved road and then 51 kilometers (32 miles) on hard-packed gravel to **Keno City,** passing **Elsa,** the site of a silver mine that closed as recently as 1989, along the way. Once a booming silver town, Keno's population has dwindled to just 20. Its long and colorful history is cataloged at the **Keno City Mining Museum** (867/995-3103, June–early Sept. daily 10 A.M.–6 P.M., donation asked for admission), fittingly housed in a 1920s saloon. The adjacent cabin has an interesting collection of locally collected fossils.

On the south side of town, **Keno City Cabins** (867/995-2829, $85–105 d)—there's only two of them—are well-equipped, with cooking done on a woodstove.

Dawson City

Of all the towns in Canada, Dawson City (not to be confused with Dawson Creek, British Columbia) has the widest fame and the wildest past. Although the Klondike gold rush was short lived, tourists have rediscovered Dawson's charms in a big way. Many historic buildings have been given cheerful coats of paint, others have very effectively been left to the ravages of Mother Nature. Walking tours are the best way to take in the history, but you can also listen to Robert Service recitals at the cabin this famous poet once called home, try your hand at panning for gold, or gamble the night away at an old-time casino.

The year-round population is around 1,400, but this almost doubles in summer. It's a long way north, some 536 kilometers (333 miles) from Whitehorse, but 60,000 visitors make the trek annually to this delightful salmagundi of colorful historic facades and abandoned buildings, tiny old cabins and huge new ones, rusted old stern-wheelers and touristy casinos.

HISTORY

The Klondike gold fields cover an area of 2,000 square kilometers (770 square miles) southeast of Dawson. It was in 1896 that a Nova Scotian prospector, Robert Henderson, discovered the first gold—about 20 cents' worth per pan—in a creek he went ahead and named Gold-Bottom Creek. He spent the rest of the summer working the creek, while passing news of his find to fellow prospectors who were in the area. One such man was George "Siwash" Washington Carmack, who with partners Tagish Charlie and Skookum Jim struck gold in extraordinary quantities—$3–4 a pan—on nearby Rabbit Creek (soon to be renamed Bonanza). They staked three claims before word began to spread. By fall most of the richest ground had been claimed.

Gold Fever

News of the strike reached the outside world a year later, when a score of prospectors, so loaded down with gold that they couldn't handle it themselves, disembarked in San Francisco and Seattle. The spectacle triggered mass insanity across the continent, immediately launching a rush the likes of which the world had rarely seen before and has not seen since. Clerks, salesmen, streetcar conductors, doctors, preachers, generals (even the mayor of Seattle) simply dropped what they were doing and started off "for the Klondike." City dwellers, factory workers, and men who had never climbed a mountain, handled a boat, or even worn a backpack were outfitted in San Francisco, Seattle, Vancouver, and Edmonton, and set out on an incredible journey through an uncharted wilderness with Dawson—a thousand miles from anywhere—as the imagined grand prize.

Out of an estimated 100,000 "stampeders" that started out, 35,000 made it to Dawson.

Meanwhile, the first few hundred lucky

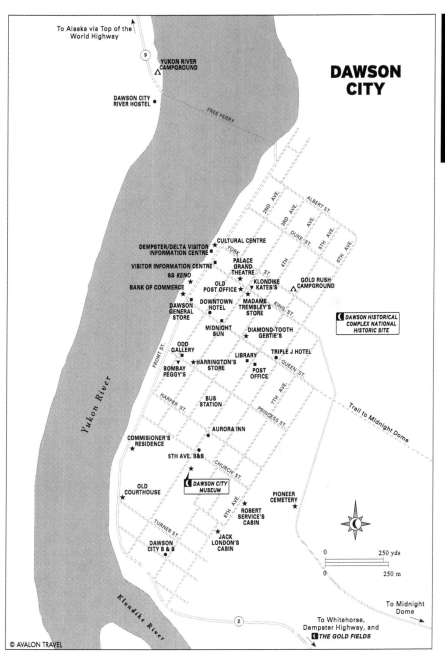

To Alaska via Top of the World Highway

YUKON RIVER CAMPGROUND

DAWSON CITY RIVER HOSTEL

FREE FERRY

DAWSON CITY

2ND AVE.
3RD AVE.
ALBERT ST.
4TH AVE.
5TH AVE.
DUKE ST.
6TH AVE.

CULTURAL CENTRE
DEMPSTER/DELTA VISITOR INFORMATION CENTRE
YORK ST.
PALACE GRAND THEATRE
VISITOR INFORMATION CENTRE
SS KENO
OLD POST OFFICE
KLONDIKE KATE'S
GOLD RUSH CAMPGROUND
BANK OF COMMERCE
DOWNTOWN HOTEL
MADAME TREMBLEY'S STORE
DAWSON GENERAL STORE
KING ST.
MIDNIGHT SUN
DIAMOND-TOOTH GERTIE'S

DAWSON HISTORICAL COMPLEX NATIONAL HISTORIC SITE

FRONT ST.
ODD GALLERY
LIBRARY
TRIPLE J HOTEL
HARRINGTON'S STORE
POST OFFICE
QUEEN ST.
BOMBAY PEGGY'S

HARPER ST.
BUS STATION
7TH AVE.
PRINCESS ST.

Yukon River

Trail to Midnight Dome

AURORA INN
COMMISSIONER'S RESIDENCE
5TH AVE. B&B
CHURCH ST.
OLD COURTHOUSE
DAWSON CITY MUSEUM
PIONEER CEMETERY
5TH AVE.
TURNER ST.
ROBERT SERVICE'S CABIN
DAWSON CITY B & B
JACK LONDON'S CABIN

0   250 yds
0   250 m

To Midnight Dome

Klondike River

To Whitehorse, Dempster Highway, and THE GOLD FIELDS

© AVALON TRAVEL

THE YUKON

stampeders to actually reach Dawson before the rivers froze that winter (1897) found the town in such a panic over food that people were actually fleeing for their lives. At the same time tens of thousands of stampeders were heading toward Dawson along a variety of routes, including over the **Chilkoot Pass** and down the Yukon River. Most hopefuls were caught unprepared in the bitter grip of the seven-month Arctic winter, and many froze to death or died of scurvy, starvation, exhaustion, heartbreak, suicide, or murder. And when the breakup in 1898 finally allowed the remaining hordes to pour into Dawson the next spring, every worthwhile claim had already been staked.

Heyday and Pay Dirt

That next year, from summer 1898 to summer 1899, was a unique moment in history. As people and supplies started deluging Dawson, all the hundreds of thousands in gold, worthless previously for lack of anything to buy, were spent with a feverish abandon. The richest stampeders established the saloons, dance halls, gambling houses, trading companies, even steamship lines and banks—much easier ways to get the gold than mining it. The casinos and hotels were as opulent as any in Paris. The dance-hall girls charged $5 in gold per minute for dancing (extra for slow dances), the bartenders put stickum on their fingers to poke a little dust during transactions, and the janitors who panned the sawdust on the barroom floors were known to wash out $50 nightly. Dawson burned with an intensity born of pure lust, the highlight of the lives of every single person who braved the trails and experienced it.

In 1899, most of Dawson burned to the ground, and at the same time, word filtered in that gold had been discovered on the beaches of Nome, and just as the Klondike strike had emptied surrounding boomtowns, Nome emptied Dawson. By the summer of 1899, as the last bedraggled and tattered stampeders limped into Dawson two years after setting out, the 12-month golden age of Dawson was done. The city's heyday was as brief as its reputation was beefy, and Dawson quickly declined

PARKS AND PARTNER'S PASS

The best way to enjoy all of Dawson's historic attractions at a reasonable price is by purchasing a Parks and Partner's Pass ($30.90 per person), which includes admission for one day to 11 local attractions as well as a guided walking tour. Passes are also available to any three attractions ($13.70) or any five attractions ($22). They can be purchased from the Visitor Reception Centre. For more information, go to www.pc.gc.ca and click through to the links for the Dawson Historical Complex National Historic Site.

into another small town on the banks of the Yukon.

SIGHTS

Dawson's plentiful free or inexpensive attractions can keep you happily busy for several days. The compact downtown area mixes dirt streets and crumbling wooden storefronts with faux gold rush–era buildings and bustling tourist businesses.

Start your exploration at the **Dawson City Visitor Information Centre** (867/993-5274, early May–late Sept. daily 10 A.M.–6 P.M., July–Aug. daily 8 A.M.–8 P.M.), right in the thick of things at Front and King Streets. Outstanding one-hour, historically loaded **walking tours** of the town core leave from the visitors center several times a day; a schedule is posted at the center.

◖ Dawson City Museum

If possible, before you do anything else in town, try to visit this excellent and extensive museum (595 5th Ave., 867/993-5291, daily 10 A.M.–6 P.M. mid-May–early Sept., adult $9, senior and child $7), housed within the imposing 1901 Administration Building. The south and north galleries present an enormous amount of history, from fossils and flora and fauna through northern Athabascan lifestyles up to the gold rush and the subsequent developments. The museum has a wealth of material to draw from and it's all nicely presented. The mining-history displays alone, from hand mining to dredges, are worth the price of admission; also check out the display on law and order during the gold rush. The "visible storage area" houses about one-fifth of the museum's collection of 30,000 artifacts.

SS *Keno*

The restored riverboat SS *Keno,* built in 1922 in Whitehorse, is beached on Front Street. It was used to transport ore from the mining area around Mayo down to the confluence of the Yukon, from where larger riverboats transported it upriver to Whitehorse and the railhead. The *Keno* sailed under its own steam to its resting place here in 1960 but wasn't restored until 40 years later. Tour cost is adult $7.50, senior $6.50, child $4.50.

Dawson Historical Complex National Historic Site

The most historically important buildings dotted around Dawson City are protected as a National Historic Site. Combine these with the most picturesque ruins of permafrost, gravity, and neglect that have purposely been left alone and you can plan on spending the best part of a day wandering around town. The following buildings are open mid-May–mid-September, with a variety interpretive programs offered at each.

On King Street, up a block from the visitors center, is the **Palace Grand Theatre,** built in 1899 from wood salvaged off stern-wheelers by "Arizona Charlie" Meadows, the most famous bartender/gunslinger on the Trail of '98. At the time, the Grand was one of the most luxuriously appointed theaters in the west, hosting everything from Wild West shows to opera. The original horseshoe balcony, private box seats, and lavish interior have been lovingly restored. Take a tour daily at 2 P.M. (adult $7.50, senior, $6.50, child $4.50).

The beautifully restored **Commissioner's Residence** on Front Street near Church Street

was the official residence of the Commissioner of the Yukon 1900–1916. Tours (adult $7.50, senior $6.50, child $4.50) of the mansion and gardens are given daily by costumed interpreters.

In the vicinity of the theater are many buildings with historic window displays. Walk three blocks south down 3rd Avenue (at Harper St.) to take a snap of the terribly slanted, oft-photographed **Strait's Auction House.**

Robert Service Cabin

Stroll three blocks uphill from the museum to 8th Avenue (at Hanson St.) to see the log cabin that Robert Service called home 1909–1912. Service, who never took shovel nor pan to earth nor water, wound up as a troubadour–bank teller in Dawson and made his fame and fortune unexpectedly while living here, penning such classic prose poems as "The Cremation of Sam McGee" and "The Shooting of Dan McGrew." No one has lived in this cabin since Service left Dawson a celebrity in 1912, and people have been making pilgrimages to it ever since. The cabin is open daily 9 A.M.–5 P.M. in the summer, and Charlie Davis does recitations of Service's best-known poems at 3 P.M. for adult $7.50, senior $6.50, child $4.50.

Midnight Dome

This 885-meter (2,900-foot) hill provides a 360-degree view of the area. The Yukon River stretches out in both directions and Dawson is right below you, to the west the Top of the World Highway winds away to Alaska, and to the south you look directly up Bonanza Creek, past the wavy tailings and hillsides pitted by hydraulic monitors that still bring pay dirt down for sluicing. The sign on top identifies all the topographic features. If you're driving, take King Street through downtown from Front Street and follow the signs; it's seven kilometers (4.3 miles) to the top. A steep hiking trail begins at the end of Queen Street (ask at the visitors center for a trail map).

The Gold Fields

For a close-up look at where the Klondike

the historic facades of Dawson City

gold frenzy took place, head two kilometers (1.2 miles) back out of town and take Bonanza Creek Road south.

The highlight of the drive is a visit to **Dredge No. 4,** the largest wooden-hulled gold dredge in North America. Built in 1912, this massive machine scooped pay dirt from the creek beds right up until 1966. Tours are offered May–August and cost adult $7.50, senior $5.50, child $4.50 (or are included in the Parks and Partner's Pass).

The Klondike Visitors Association owns **Claim 6** on the famous Bonanza Creek. You can pan for gold free of charge mid-May–mid-September. Buy a pan from any one of many shops in Dawson or rent one from the RV park at the Bonanza Creek Road turn-off. Downstream a ways, **Claim 33** (867/993-5303) is a commercial panning operation where you pay a small fee to pan for guaranteed "color." Hope I'm not giving away any secrets, but it's spiked. Still, it's good fun and a way to practice your technique.

A monument at **Discovery Claim,** 16 kilometers (10 miles) south from the main highway, marks the spot where George Carmack made the strike in 1896 that set the rush into motion.

The road continues beyond the monument to the confluence of Bonanza and Eldorado Creeks, site of the gold-rush town of Grand Forks, and then splits. The left fork is part of a 100-kilometer (62-mile) loop through some seriously isolated country before rejoining the Klondike Highway near the airport.

ENTERTAINMENT

Canada's first legal casino, **Diamond Tooth Gerties** (4th and Queen, 867/993-5575, early May–mid-Sept. Sun.–Wed. 7 P.M.–2 A.M. and Thurs.–Sat. 2 P.M.–2 A.M.), was named for a Dawson dance-hall queen with a diamond between her two front teeth. Though casinos were as common as sluice boxes and saloons at the height of the Dawson madness, gambling in the Yukon (and throughout Canada) wasn't formally legalized until 1971, the year this place opened. Games include slot machines, blackjack, poker, sic bo, and roulette, with odds

ONLY IN THE NORTH ...

Dawson's most infamous nightcap can be "enjoyed" at the **Downtown Hotel** (Queen St. and 2nd Ave., 867/993-5346). It all began in 1973 when "Captain" Dick Stevenson was searching though an abandoned cabin and he came across a pickle jar that held a toe that had been severed by an ax. Inspiration (if it could be called that) struck, and the toe landed in a drink. The original toe is long gone – it was swallowed by an overzealous patron – but at last check, the bar in the Downtown Hotel had eight toes to choose from, all looking ghastly at best. They're preserved in salt, and came from donations by folks who lost them in accidents or because of frostbite. It's pretty gross, but amazingly popular – 2,000 or so folks become members of the **Sourtoe Cocktail Club** annually. Sourtoe cocktails are $5 (you can put the toe in any drink). The bartenders make sure the toe touches your lip to receive an official certificate showing your prowess in stupid bar tricks.

that decidedly favor the house. Drinks are not free, even if you're dropping major-league cash. This sure isn't Vegas! The 30-minute floorshow of Geritol oldies and cancan kicks is presented nightly at 8:30 P.M., 10:30 P.M., and midnight. Cover charge is $10.

Gerties is run by the Klondike Visitors Association as a money-maker to restore and promote Dawson City. Take a look around town and you'll see how much money they make at Gerties (or how much the tourists lose)—around $1 million annually. I'm not saying that you won't come out in front, but just approach this joint with the attitude that you're making a donation. And why not? It's for a very good cause.

SHOPPING

The Klondike Institute of Art and Culture operates the **Odd Gallery** (2nd Ave. and Princess St., 867/993-5005), which hosts exhibits of art by Yukoners. This association also organizes the mid-August **Yukon Riverside Arts Festival** beside the Yukon River as it flows past downtown. **Art's Gallery** (3rd Ave. and King St., 867/993-6967) sells excellent hand-blown art glass, scrimshaw, pottery, batiks, and baskets woven from birch, cedar, or spruce root.

The most interesting of touristy Dawson's many gift shops is the **Gold Claim** (3rd Ave. and Princess St., 867/993-6387) operated by Stuart Schmidt, whose grandfather was one of the original Klondikers. Schmidt uses gold he's mined himself to make hand-forged jewelry. **Fortymile Gold Placers** (3rd Ave. and York St., 867/993-5690) is in the business of selling and buying claims, but also sells raw gold out of its offices.

ACCOMMODATIONS AND CAMPING

Check the **Klondike Visitors Association** website (www.dawsoncity.ca) for a complete list of local lodgings. If you arrive in Dawson without reservations, be sure to check out the lodging notebook in the Visitor Information Centre; often hotels, motels, and bed-and-breakfasts will advertise special rates for the night here.

Under $50

◖ **Dawson City River Hostel** (867/993-6823, www.yukonhostels.com, mid-May–Sept.) is Canada's northernmost hostel. Located on the west side of the Yukon, it's a quick ferry ride from Dawson. A back-to-the-land spirit infuses this friendly place where dorm-style lodging in cabins is $18 for members of Hostelling International (nonmembers $22), private rooms are $46 s or d, and tent spaces cost $14 s, $23 d. The hostel doesn't have electricity (and therefore it's cash only), but does have a cooking area with woodstove, canoe and mountain bike rentals, a communal cabin, plus the funkiest bathhouse going.

$50-100

The cheapest place right downtown is the

shockingly pink **Westminster Hotel** (975 3rd Ave., 867/993-5463, www.thewestminsterhotel-1898.com), where basic rooms with shared bath go for $45–55 s, $55–65 d. The Westminster is definitely not for everyone and it helps to be a heavy sleeper, as the downstairs bar gets noisy Friday–Saturday when the country house band gets going.

If you really want to immerse yourself in the gold-mining culture of Dawson, consider staying at a camp set up by **Eureka Gold Panning Adventures** (867/633-6519, www.eurekagoldpanning.com) beyond Bonanza Creek Road along Hunker Creek. Morris and Sandy George supply wall tents, cooking facilities, wood-burning heaters, and solar showers. You supply sleeping bags and food. Rates are $60 s, $75 d, but most visitors stay as part of a package, such as $100 per person for one night accommodation and two full days of gold-panning. Round-trip transportation from Dawson, if required, is $60 for one person, $85 for two.

$100-150

In addition to having great breakfasts, **Klondike Kate's** (3rd and King, 867/993-6527, www.klondikekates.ca, Apr.–Sept., $100–140 s, $120–160 d) has 15 spacious wood cabins, each with a bathroom, cable TV, free Internet, and a phone.

Next to the museum, **5th Avenue B&B** (867/993-5941 or 866/631-5237, www.5thavebandb.com, $95–125 s, $105–135 d) may have an uninspiring name but the aquamarine exterior is impossible to miss. It features seven comfortable guest rooms with shared or private baths and a large sitting area. Rates include all-you-can-eat continental breakfast.

Across from Diamond Tooth Gertie's is the **Triple J Hotel** (5th and Queen, 867/993-5323 or 800/764-3555, www.triplejhotel.com, mid-May–mid-Sept.), a gold rush–era–looking hotel that, beyond the facade, is a modern complex of motel rooms ($132 s, $142 d), hotel rooms ($132 s, $142 d), and cabins ($142 s, $152 d).

Fun and funky on the outside, the rooms at

the **Downtown Hotel** (Queen at 2nd, 867/993-5346 or 867/993-5346, www.downtownhotel.ca, $118 s, $133 d) are somewhat clinical. Still, it's close to everything and the on-site bar has a rocking nighttime atmosphere.

Over $150

On the outskirts of town and less than a block from the Klondike River, **Dawson City B&B** (451 Craig St., 867/993-5649, www.dawsonbb.com, $165 s or d) is a neat two-story home with a pleasing blue and white exterior. Rates include a cooked breakfast, bikes, fishing poles, and airport transfers.

The **Aurora Inn** (5th Ave., 867/993-6860, www.aurorainn.ca, $149 s, $169–199 d) is a modern wooden lodging with a distinctive yellow facade. The rooms are bright and spacious, with simple furnishings and practical bathrooms.

Bombay Peggy's Inn & Pub (2nd at Princess, 867/993-6969, www.bombaypeggys.com, $169–189 s, $179–199 d) is named for the former madam of a brothel that once operated in the building. Not only has it been totally renovated, it was moved from its original location. Most rooms are decorated in bold Victorian colors, with hardwood floors and lavish bathrooms with antique tubs. You don't have to abandon modern comforts for the sake of atmosphere—there's also high-speed Internet. Rates include a light breakfast. About the only reminders of the building's previous use are a racy cocktail list in the downstairs lounge and the phone number. It's also one of the few Dawson lodgings open year-round.

Camping

Yukon River Campground (across the river from town, mid-May–mid-Sept., $15) is convenient but lacks amenities (drinking water, pit toilets, and firewood only). The free ferry from town runs 24 hours daily. Walk downstream from the campground to reach three rusting riverboats that are slowly disintegrating where they were beached many years ago.

RVers can circle their rigs right downtown

at the **Goldrush Campground** (5th and York, 867/993-5247, www.goldrushcampground. com, mid-May–mid-Sept., unserviced sites $19, hookups $31.50–38.50). Amenities include coin showers, a laundry, and wireless Internet throughout. South of town, **Bonanza Gold RV Park** (867/993-6789 or 888/993-6789, www.bonanzagold.ca, tents $10, hookups $23–39) has modern facilities, but tents are not permitted.

FOOD

Dawson is great for eating out; check the menu book at the Visitor Information Centre to see which places look inviting.

Riverwest Bistro Restaurant (Front St., 867/993-6339, daily from 7:30 A.M.) has good coffee plus a deli with the best sandwiches in town, and a delightful selection of baked goods.

The breakfast special at ◖ **Klondike Kate's** (3rd Ave. and King St., 867/993-6527, April–Sept. daily 6:30 A.M.–11 P.M., $14–24) isn't as legendary as the restaurant's namesake was during the gold rush, but it's still mighty popular. Bacon and eggs with baked beans and home fries will set you back $9. Pancakes and omelets are similarly priced. At lunch, salads and gourmet sandwiches are all under $15, while at dinner, plan on starting with prawns in ouzo ($11), and go on to pan-seared arctic char ($23). This place has a warm ambience and Dawson's nicest patio.

Groceries

Dawson City General Store (540 Front St., 867/993-5813, daily 8 A.M.–9 P.M.) has a bakery and groceries, but your best bet for fresh meat and deli items is the **Bonanza Market** (2nd and Princess, 867/993-6567, Mon.–Sat. 9 A.M.–7 P.M.).

INFORMATION

The centrally located **Dawson City Visitor Information Centre** (Front St. and King St., 867/993-5274, early May–late Sept. daily 10 A.M.–6 P.M., July–Aug. daily 8 A.M.–8 P.M.) is extremely well organized and prepared for the most common questions from the hordes of hopefuls that are, after all, Dawson's legacy. It stocks books of menus, hotel rates, and gift shops; schedules of tours; hours of attractions; and much, much more. Additionally, the **Klondike Visitors Association** (867/993-5575 or 877/465-3006, www.dawsoncity.ca) has a website filled with useful information.

The library is at 5th and Queen in the same building as the public school (remove your shoes before entering). **Maximillian's Gold Rush Emporium** (Front St., 867/993-5486) has a great selection of northern literature. One of the most unique souvenirs you can get in Dawson is an authentic **placer map** showing all the gold fields and claims. They are available along with topo maps at the **mining recorder's office** (5th Ave. between Queen St. and Princess St.).

GETTING THERE

Dawson is accessible from the south via the year-round **North Klondike Highway** (536 km/333 mi from Whitehorse), with westward connections to Alaska over the seasonal **Top of the World Highway** (280 km/174 mi to Tok, Alaska).

Dawson's airport is 17 kilometers (10.6 miles) east of town. **Air North** (867/668-2228) links Dawson with Inuvik and Whitehorse, with direct connections south to Vancouver, Calgary, and Edmonton from the capital. Taxis and a shuttle bus meet all flights.

Alaska/Yukon Trails (888/600-6001, www. alaskashuttle.com) has a thrice-weekly summer bus service connecting Dawson City with Whitehorse ($149) and Fairbanks (US$169).

CONTINUING WEST TO ALASKA

If you arrived in Dawson City by road from Whitehorse, you have the option of returning the way you came or continuing to Alaska along the Top of the World Highway. If you arrived in town by public transportation, your options are a little more varied—fly or bus it out in either direction or catch the *Yukon Queen* to Eagle.

DEMPSTER HIGHWAY

Dawson is the jumping off point for the 741-kilometer (460-mile) Dempster Highway that leads across the **Arctic Circle** to **Inuvik** in the Northwest Territories. Unpaved all the way, it traverses endless tundra and snowcapped mountain ranges; it crosses the migration path of the Porcupine caribou herd; and, in winter, you can drive clear through to the **Arctic Ocean** on the frozen Mackenzie River. But it's also one of the most remote public roads in North America, one for which you must be prepared with a full gas tank and spare tires. You also need to turn around at the end and return to Dawson along the same route.

DRIVING THE DEMPSTER

Request information packages from either of the territorial tourism bureaus before leaving home, then make a stop at the **Dempster/Delta Visitor Information Centre** (Front St., Dawson City, 867/993-6167, mid-May-mid-Sept. daily 9 A.M.-8 P.M.). The ferry crossing of the Peel River operates mid-June-October. For a schedule and general highway conditions call 800/661-0750 or go online to www.dot.gov.nt.ca.

Numerous campgrounds and three lodges dot the route. A good spot to spend the night before hitting the highway is **Klondike River Lodge** (867/993-6892), east of Dawson at the start of the highway. Tent sites are $12, hookups $28, and motel rooms $135 s or d. They also have gas pumps and a small restaurant. The **Arctic Circle** is reached at Kilometer 403 (Mile 250) and the Yukon/Northwest Territories border at Kilometer 471 (Mile 293). **Fort McPherson,** 550 kilometers (342 miles) from Dawson, is a Gwich'in Dene village of 800 with a visitors center and other highway services.

Top of the World Highway

Heading west toward Alaska, the Top of the World Highway crosses the Yukon River at the edge of Dawson. A free **ferry,** with room for up to eight regular-sized vehicles, crosses the Yukon River mid-May–mid-September, on demand 24 hours a day (except Wed. 5–7 A.M.). It's a fun ride even if you're not heading up the Top of the World Highway.

From the west bank of the Yukon, the highway climbs out of Dawson into the alpine tundra of the lower White Mountains, with vast vistas in which you can see the road running along the ridge tops in the distance. Civilization along the highway, however, is nonexistent until you reach **Poker Creek, Alaska** at Kilometer 106 (Mile 66). With a population of two, this is the northernmost border station in the United States. It's open for as long as the Dawson car ferry operates (usually mid-May–mid-Sept.), daily 9 A.M.–9 P.M. After crossing into Alaska, you must also turn your watch *back* one hour to Alaska Time (which means if you're traveling to Dawson from Alaska, the border station is open daily 8 A.M.–8 P.M.).

Note: The Dawson ferry can get heavily backed up in mid-summer, with delays of up to two hours at the busiest times (7–11 A.M. and 4–7 P.M.). Don't head off too late in the day if you intend to make the border crossing before it closes.

NORTHWEST TERRITORIES

One of three Canadian territories (the Yukon and Nunavut are the other two), the Northwest Territories is a vast wilderness of uncompromising nature. Stretching from the 60th parallel across the Arctic Circle and into the High Arctic, it takes in some of the world's biggest and deepest lakes, the massive Mackenzie River, and treeless tundra that seemingly extends forever. Although the Northwest Territories is vast, many of the highlights are accessible by air or road, including one route leading north through Northern Alberta from Grimshaw. Whether it's your first time or your 40th, crossing the 60th parallel into the Northwest Territories marks the beginning of a new adventure. And for road travelers, the adventure starts in the most accessible section of the territories,

along the Waterfalls Route through a vast expanse of stunted boreal forest broken only by two of North America's largest rivers, the Slave and Mackenzie. To the north lies Great Slave Lake, named for the Slavey Dene who have trapped and fished along its southern shores for thousands of years. This vast inland freshwater sea is the world's 10th-largest lake. The region's main communities are Hay River, on the south shore of Great Slave Lake; and Fort Smith, the gateway to Wood Buffalo National Park, the second-largest national park in the world. Paved and improved gravel roads link the two towns and continue around the west and north sides of Great Slave Lake to the city of Yellowknife, known as the "Diamond Capital of North America." From this point, it's air travel only north to

© ANDREW HEMPSTEAD

NORTHWEST TERRITORIES

HIGHLIGHTS

◖ Wood Buffalo National Park: A visit to the world's second largest national park requires time and patience, but visitors will be rewarded with the sight of the world's largest free-roaming herd of bison (page 45).

◖ Prince of Wales Northern Heritage Centre: Yellowknife's premier attraction lays out the entire natural and human history of the territory in a modern, inviting lakefront setting (page 48).

◖ Yellowknife's Old Town: Park your car and explore one of western Canada's most eccentric neighborhoods on foot, taking time out for a meal at the utterly unique Wildcat Cafe (page 50).

◖ Golfing Under the Midnight Sun: There's no such thing as twilight rates at the Yellowknife Golf Club, where it's possible to tee off day and night in late June and early July (page 51).

◖ Nahanni National Park: A day trip by floatplane is fine, but a guided trip down the South Nahanni River is what draws most visitors to this remote and mountainous park (page 56).

◖ Tuktoyaktuk: If you're the type that needs to see what's at the end of the road, you won't want to miss "Tuk," a tiny village perched on the edge of the Arctic Ocean, but made accessible for all with day trips from Inuvik (page 64).

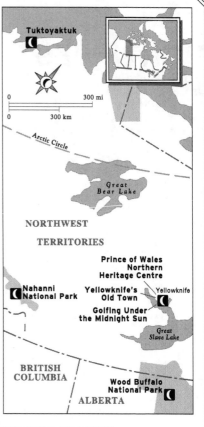

LOOK FOR ◖ TO FIND RECOMMENDED SIGHTS, ACTIVITIES, DINING, AND LODGING.

two of the world's 10 largest lakes, one of the world's longest rivers, a waterfall twice the height of Niagara Falls, one UNESCO World Heritage Site, three more national parks, and an amazing abundance of wildlife. Hiking the Canol Road, canoeing the South Nahanni River, fishing for trophy-size lake trout in Great Bear Lake, and watching beluga whales frolic in the Beaufort Sea are just the highlights.

PLANNING YOUR TIME

Heading to the Northwest Territories is not to be taken lightly. You will need to plan ahead, especially if you have a specific activity in mind, such as joining a guided rafting trip through Nahanni National Park, which requires booking well in advance and making the relevant transportation bookings. Those driving north from Alberta should allow at least one week in the Northwest Territories. This is enough

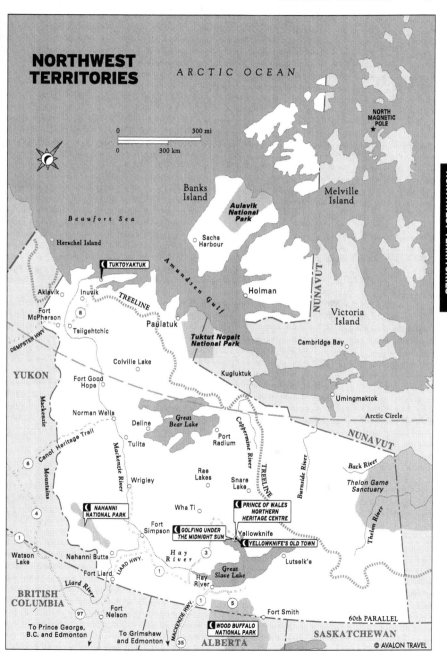

NORTHWEST TERRITORIES

NORTHWEST TERRITORIES

ARCTIC OCEAN

NORTH MAGNETIC POLE ★

0   300 mi
0   300 km

Banks Island

Melville Island

Aulavik National Park

Beaufort Sea

Herschel Island

Sachs Harbour

TUKTOYAKTUK

Amundsen Gulf

Aklavik

Inuvik

TREELINE

Holman

Fort McPherson

8

Tsiigehtchic

Paulatuk

Victoria Island

DEMPSTER HWY.

Tuktut Nogait National Park

Cambridge Bay

YUKON

Colville Lake

Kugluktuk

NUNAVUT

Fort Good Hope

Umingmaktok

Arctic Circle

Norman Wells

Deline

Great Bear Lake

Coppermine River

NUNAVUT

Mackenzie

Canol Heritage Trail

6

Tulita

Port Radium

TREELINE

Burnside River

Back River

Thelon Game Sanctuary

Mountains

Mackenzie River

Wrigley

Rae Lakes

Snare Lake

4

Wha Ti

PRINCE OF WALES NORTHERN HERITAGE CENTRE

Thelon River

NAHANNI NATIONAL PARK

Fort Simpson

GOLFING UNDER THE MIDNIGHT SUN

Yellowknife

1

Watson Lake

Nahanni Butte

LIARD HWY.

Hay River

3

YELLOWKNIFE'S OLD TOWN

Lutsel'e

Fort Liard

1

Great Slave Lake

BRITISH COLUMBIA

Liard River

Hay River

1

97

Fort Nelson

5

Fort Smith

60th PARALLEL

To Prince George, B.C. and Edmonton

To Grimshaw and Edmonton

MACKENZIE HWY.

35

WOOD BUFFALO NATIONAL PARK

ALBERTA

SASKATCHEWAN

© AVALON TRAVEL

time to see the abundant natural wonders of Wood Buffalo National Park before heading to the capital of Yellowknife, where two days is enough time to see the Prince of Wales Northern Heritage Centre, wander through Old Town, try your hand at fishing, and go paddling in one of the many surrounding lakes. If it's late June, golfing under the midnight sun is a once-in-a-lifetime experience, but the local links is worth hitting at any time of the summer. Backtracking from the capital, head west to Fort Simpson for a flightseeing day trip into Nahanni National Park. Exiting the Northwest Territories at Fort Liard will set you up for another week's worth of adventures in northern British Columbia and the Yukon.

If you're keen to travel above the Arctic Circle, it is possible to combine a driving tour to Yellowknife with a flight to Inuvik. The town itself is interesting, but it's the prospect of experiencing a sun that never sets (in late June) or seeing—or swimming in, for the brave—the Arctic Ocean on a side trip to Tuktoyaktuk that brings most visitors this far north. The ideal scenario would be to book a three-night stay, flying up from Yellowknife (or Calgary or Edmonton) to Inuvik, with one full day to explore town and another to visit "Tuk." Travelers with reliable vehicles can also reach Inuvik by road through the Yukon. Allow at least four days for the round-trip from Dawson City.

Waterfalls Route

Named for the many waterfalls in the accessible south-central portion of the Northwest Territories, this region is reached by road from northern Alberta and provides the gateway to Yellowknife. The largest population center is Hay River, on the southern shore of Great Slave Lake.

60TH PARALLEL TO HAY RIVER

The wood-and-stone structure marking the 60th parallel is a welcome sight after the long drive north through northern Alberta up the Mackenzie Highway. North of the border, the highway number changes from 35 to 1, and the road follows the Hay River 118 kilometers (73 miles) to Great Slave Lake. This stretch is known as the **Waterfalls Route,** for the impressive falls along the way.

Just beyond the border is the **60th Parallel Visitors Centre** (867/875-5570, mid-May–mid-Sept. daily 8:30 A.M.–8:30 P.M.), well worth a stop just to have a chat with the friendly hosts. The center offers maps and brochures, camping permits, fishing licenses, and displays of local arts and crafts. And the coffeepot is always on, accompanied by freshly

made scones, if you're lucky. Behind the center is the **60th Parallel Campground** (mid-May–mid-Sept., unserviced sites $15), a small facility beside the Hay River.

Twin Falls Gorge Territorial Park

North of the border, the Hay River has carved a deep gorge into the limestone bedrock. Punctuating the river's flow are two dramatic waterfalls that formed a major barrier for early river travelers, forcing a portage along the west bank. Encompassing both falls, and equally impressive, is Twin Falls Gorge Territorial Park. From the first day-use area, a short trail leads to a viewing platform overlooking **Alexandra Falls,** where the peat-colored Hay River tumbles 34 meters (112 feet). **Louise Falls,** three kilometers (1.9 miles) downstream, is not as high, but its intriguing steps make it just as interesting. **Louise Falls Campground** (mid-May–mid-Sept., unserviced sites $17) has water, pit toilets, and bug-proof cooking shelters.

HAY RIVER

This town of 3,600 lies 118 kilometers (73 miles) north of the border, 1,070 kilometers

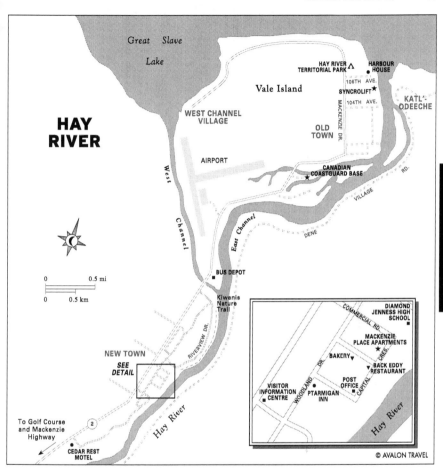

HAY RIVER

Great Slave Lake

Vale Island

HAY RIVER TERRITORIAL PARK

HARBOUR HOUSE

106TH AVE.

SYNCROLIFT

104TH AVE.

MACKENZIE DR.

KATL'-ODEECHE

WEST CHANNEL VILLAGE

OLD TOWN

West

AIRPORT

CANADIAN COASTGUARD BASE

Channel

East Channel

VILLAGE

RD.

DENE

BUS DEPOT

Kiwanis Nature Trail

0   0.5 mi
0   0.5 km

RIVERVIEW DR.

NEW TOWN

SEE DETAIL

Hay River

To Golf Course and Mackenzie Highway
2

CEDAR REST MOTEL

COMMERCIAL RD.

DIAMOND JENNESS HIGH SCHOOL

MACKENZIE PLACE APARTMENTS

CRES.

BAKERY

BACK EDDY RESTAURANT

WOODLAND DR.

CAPITAL

VISITOR INFORMATION CENTRE

POST OFFICE

PTARMIGAN INN

Hay River

© AVALON TRAVEL

(665 miles) north of Edmonton and 500 kilometers (310 miles) from the territorial capital of Yellowknife. Hay River is a vital transportation link for waterborne freight bound for communities along the Mackenzie River and throughout the western and central Arctic.

Within the town limits, several distinct communities surround the delta, which was formed where the Hay River flows into Great Slave Lake. Most modern development, including motels, restaurants, and government offices, is located in **New Town,** on the west bank of the Hay River. A bridge links New Town to **Vale Island,** where the airport, campground, and excellent beaches are located. Also on the island are the communities of **Old Town,** which was partially destroyed by flooding in 1963, and **West Channel Village,** which grew around the commercial fishing industry. Across the mouth of Hay River is Katl'odeeche (Hay River Dene Reserve), the only native reserve in the Northwest Territories.

Sights

To get oriented, head to the manager's office (2nd floor) at the 17-story **Mackenzie Place**

Apartment Building. Ask for a key and ride the claustrophobia-inducing elevator to the roof, where panoramic views of the Great Slave Lake, Hay River, and the boreal forest extend to the horizon. The **Diamond Jenness Secondary School** (Riverview Dr.) was named for a famed Northern anthropologist and is undoubtedly the town's most unusual structure. It was designed by Douglas Cardinal, an Albertan architect whose distinctive work is found throughout that province. Its curved walls alone would have made it a Northern landmark, but the choice of color for the entire exterior was left to the students—and they chose purple! (It's known to locals as the "Purple People Eater.") Behind the school, the **Kiwanis Nature Trail** leads along the west bank of the Hay River (look for fossils) to various signposted points of interest, then across Highway 2 and along the West Channel to Great Slave Lake.

The boarded-up shop fronts, dusty streets, and empty houses of **Vale Island** belie the activity that still takes place along the waterfront. The large **Canadian Coast Guard Base** is responsible for all search-and-rescue operations in the western Arctic. And the facilities of the **Northern Transportation Company Ltd.** (NTCL), a large shipping concern, include shipyards, a dry dock, freight-storage areas, and a syncrolift—a hydraulic device that removes vessels from the water for easy maintenance (it's one of only four in Canada; it can be seen to the right along 106th Ave.).

From Old Town, Mackenzie Drive—the island's main thoroughfare—continues past a popular swimming beach and a radio observatory before it dead-ends in **West Channel Village,** a once-prosperous fishing community.

Recreation

The beaches of Vale Island are very popular during summer, even if the water may be a little cold for most southerners. The best beach is within **Hay River Territorial Park** at the end of 106th Avenue, although those farther around the island are quieter. Anglers will find plentiful northern pike and pickerel in the Hay River.

Hay River Golf Club (13 km/eight mi south

The Diamond Jenness Secondary School is a local landmark.

of town, 867/874-6290) is the finest course in the territory. It has nine holes with grassed fairways, artificial greens, a driving range, and a superbly crafted log clubhouse (well worth a look, even for non-golfers). A round of golf (18 holes) is $40. The course also has a driving range, and club rentals are available.

Accommodations and Camping

The seven-room **Harbour House Bed and Breakfast** (106th St., 867/874-2233, www. greenwayrealty.ca, $80 s, $90 d) is an excellent choice for accommodations in Hay River. Across from Vale Island's best beach, the setting is wonderful and the mood casual. Rates include a full breakfast.

A couple of kilometers (1.2 miles) south from downtown is **Cedar Rest Motel** (938 Mackenzie Hwy., 867/874-3732, $95 s, $105 d), a place that looks half finished, with a massive gravel parking lot out front broken by a gas station. At the centrally located **Ptarmigan Inn** (867/874-6781 or 800/661-0842, www.ptarmiganinn.com, $134–179 s or d), rooms are air-conditioned and have high-speed Internet access.

Hay River Territorial Park (867/874-3772, Vale Island, mid-May–mid-Sept., $17–21) is a short walk from the beach and seven kilometers (4.3 miles) from downtown. The 35 sites are private, a few have power, and all have picnic tables and fire rings.

Food

Beside Northern, **Hay River Bakery** (867/874-2322, Mon.–Fri. 8 A.M.–6 P.M.) has a wide variety of cakes and pastries and is a good place for an inexpensive lunch.

Keys Dining Room (Ptarmigan Inn, 867/874-6781, Mon.–Sat. 7 A.M.–9 P.M., Sun. 8 A.M.–9 P.M., $16–29) is your typical hotel restaurant, with something for everyone (think stir-fries, pastas, beef), as well as locally caught whitefish. Worth the effort to find is **Back Eddy Restaurant** (6 Courtoreille St., 867/874-6680, Mon.–Fri. 11 A.M.–2 P.M. and 5–9 P.M., Sat. 11 A.M.–10 P.M., $15–27), above Rings Drug Store on Capital Crescent. Meals are served in the lounge or, for families, in a separate dining area. The menu features pickerel and whitefish fresh from the lake.

Information

Hay River Visitor Information Centre (73 Woodland Dr., 867/874-3180, www.hayriver. com, mid-May–mid-Sept. daily 9 A.M.–9 P.M.) is at the south entrance to town. It has bundles of brochures and books, and, almost as importantly, the coffeepot is always on. **Hay River Centennial Library** (75 Woodland Dr., 867/874-6486, Mon.–Thurs. 10 A.M.–5 P.M., Fri.–Sun. 1–5 P.M.) has free wireless Internet.

Getting There

Hay River Airport is on Vale Island, a $15 cab ride from town. During freeze-up and breakup of the Mackenzie River, road traffic through to Yellowknife is blocked, and Hay River Airport becomes the center of frenzied activity; freight and passengers arriving by road from the south transfer to planes for the short hop over Great Slave Lake. **First Air** (800/267-1247, www. firstair.ca) flies once or twice daily between Hay River and Yellowknife.

The bus depot is at the south end of Vale Island. **Greyhound** departs daily for Edmonton (16 hours). Connecting with the Greyhound services is **Frontier Coachlines** (867/873-4892), using the same depot.

HAY RIVER TO FORT SMITH

The 270-kilometer (168 miles) road linking Hay River to Fort Smith (Hwy. 5) is paved for the first 60 kilometers (37 miles) then turns to improved gravel. No services are available along this route. A gravel road to the north, 49 kilometers (30 miles) from Highway 2, leads two kilometers (1.2 miles) to **Polar Lake.** The lake is stocked with rainbow trout and has good bird-watching around the shoreline.

Another 11 kilometers (6.8 miles) beyond the Polar Lake turn-off, the highway divides: The right fork continues to Fort Smith, the left to Fort Resolution.

Fort Resolution

This historic community of 470 is in a forested

PINE POINT: A MODERN GHOST TOWN

In 1951 the mining giant Cominco began extracting lead and zinc from an open-pit mine east of Hay River at a site known as Pine Point. With production on the increase, a town was built, at one time boasting more than 2,000 residents. Low lead and zinc prices, coupled with rising operational costs, forced Cominco to close the mine in 1988. One of the lease conditions was that Cominco was to restore the land to its original condition when it left. As a result, the whole town – a school, a hospital, a supermarket, and hundreds of houses – had to be moved. After standing empty for a few years, the buildings were moved to various locations throughout the north. Today all that remains are tailing piles from the mine, paved streets, sidewalks, and a golf course with a rough that makes the U.S. Open look tame.

area on the shore of Great Slave Lake around 170 kilometers (106 miles) east of Hay River. The original fort, built by the North West Company in 1786, was to the east, on the Slave River Delta. When the post was moved, a Chipewyan Dene settlement grew around it, and in 1852 Roman Catholic missionaries arrived, building a school and a hospital. A road connecting the town to Pine Point was completed in the 1960s, and today the mainly Chipewyan and Métis population relies on trapping and a sawmill operation as its economic base.

Continuing to Fort Smith on Highway 5

From the Fort Smith/Fort Resolution junction, 60 kilometers (33 miles) east of Hay River, it's another 210 kilometers (130 miles) southeast to Fort Smith. After an hour of smooth sailing, the road enters **Wood Buffalo National Park,** the largest national park in North America. Five kilometers (3.1 miles) beyond the park entrance sign is the **Angus Fire Tower.** Behind the tower is one of many sinkholes found in the northern reaches of the park. This example of karst topography occurs when underground caves collapse, creating a craterlike depression. This one is 26 meters (85 feet) deep and 40 meters (130 feet) across. The next worthwhile stop is at **Nyarling River,** 14 kilometers (8.7 miles) farther east. The dried-up riverbed is actually the path of an underground river, hence the name *Nyarling* (underground, in the Slavey language).

As the highway continues east, it enters an area where the Precambrian Shield is exposed, making for a rocky landscape where stunted trees cling to shallow depressions that have filled with soil. To the north, an access road leads to several small waterfalls in **Little Buffalo Falls Territorial Park** and a campground (mid-May–mid-Sept., $17) with pit toilets, a kitchen shelter, and firewood.

FORT SMITH

Until 1967, this town of 2,300 was the territorial capital. It still functions as an administrative center for various governmental offices and is the educational center for the Northwest Territories. The town was established because of formidable rapids on the Slave River, a vital link for all travelers heading north. In 1872, the Hudson's Bay Company opened a post, later known as Fort Fitzgerald, at the southern end of the rapids. Two years later, the company established a fort near the northern end of the portage route, at Fort Smith.

Sights

Most people who venture to Fort Smith do so to visit Wood Buffalo National Park, but there are a couple of interesting sights within town limits.

In the 1920s, when Fort Smith was the capital of the Northwest Territories, administrative duties fell to the local bishop, whose house and gardens are now part of **Fort Smith Mission Historic Park** (corner of Mercredi Ave. and Breynat St., 867/874-6702, free). Declared a

Territorial Historic Park in 1991, it's an ongoing restoration project; at this stage, interpretive signs explain the various buildings, and gardens are planted for each summer. The fort-shaped **Northern Life Museum** (110 King St., 867/872-2859, daily 1–5 P.M. June–Aug., free) houses many artifacts collected by early missionaries, including dog-mushing equipment, Inuit carvings, and the first printing press in the north. Along the riverfront on Marine Drive is the **Slave River Lookout.** Use the spotting scope here to search out white pelicans nesting on rocks scattered through the river.

Accommodations and Camping

Thebacha Bed & Breakfast (53 Portage Ave., 867/872-2060, www.taigatour.com, $80 s, $100 d) offers four guest rooms, breakfast, and the use of a kitchen in a centrally located residence. For motel accommodations, consider **Pelican Rapids Inn** (152 McDougal Rd., 867/872-2789, $140 s or d), with 31 basic but spacious rooms.

The only campground close to town is the **Queen Elizabeth Territorial Park,** four kilometers (2.5 miles) west toward the airport; turn north on Teepee Trail Road. Sites cost $17 per night and are spread out and private, with pit toilets and cooking shelters. Showers and flush toilets are available in the warden's compound.

◖ WOOD BUFFALO NATIONAL PARK

From Fort Smith, Highway 5 continues through town and loops back south into Alberta (just beyond town limits). The border is also the northern boundary of Wood Buffalo National Park, the second largest national park in the world (the largest is in Greenland). Throughout this 45,000-square-kilometer (17,400-square-mile) chunk of boreal forest, boreal plains, shallow lakes, and bogs flow two major rivers—the Peace and Athabasca. These drain into **Lake Claire,** forming one of the world's largest freshwater deltas. The Peace-Athabasca Delta is a mass of confusing channels, shallow lakes, and sedge

Salt Plains at Wood Buffalo National Park

NORTHWEST TERRITORIES

WHOOPING CRANES

Through a successful captive-breeding program, the whooping crane, *Grus americana,* has become a symbol of human efforts to protect endangered species in North America. Whoopers, as they are commonly called, have never been prolific. They stand 1.3 meters (four feet), have a wingspan of 2.4 meters (eight feet), and are pure white with long black legs. (They are often confused with the slightly smaller, reddish-brown sandhill crane, which is common in the park.) Their naturally low reproduction rate, coupled with severe degradation of their habitat, caused their numbers to dip to as low as 21 in 1954 – a single flock nested in Wood Buffalo National Park. Today, the population of the highly publicized and heavily studied flock has increased to more than 350, more than half the number that remain worldwide (most of the others are in captivity). The birds nest in a remote area of marshes and bogs in the northern reaches of Wood Buffalo far from human contact, migrating south to the Texas coast each fall.

meadows, surrounded by a wetland that is a prime wintering range for bison, rich in waterfowl, and home to beavers, muskrats, moose, lynx, wolves, and black bears. From the delta, the Slave River, which forms the park's eastern boundary, flows north into Great Slave Lake.

Probably best known for being the last natural nesting habitat of the rare whooping crane, the park is also home to the world's largest free-roaming herd of bison. It has extensive salt plains and North America's finest example of gypsum karst topography—a phenomenon created by underground water activity. For all of these reasons, and as an intact example of the boreal forest that once circled the entire Northern Hemisphere, the park was declared a UNESCO World Heritage Site in December 1983.

Sights

The expansive **Salt Plains** in the northeast of the park are one of Wood Buffalo's dominant natural features. Underground water flows through deposits of salt left behind by an ancient saltwater ocean, emerging in the form of salt springs. Large white mounds form at their source, and where the water has evaporated the ground is covered in a fine layer of salt. The best place to view this phenomenon is from the **Salt Plains Overlook,** 35 kilometers (22 miles) west of Fort Smith, then 11 kilometers (6.8 miles) south on Parson's Lake Road. The panoramic view of the plains is spectacular from this spot, but it's worth taking the one-kilometer (0.6-mile) trail to the bottom of the hill.

In the same vicinity, a bedrock of **gypsum karst** underlies much of the park. Gypsum is a soft, white rock that slowly dissolves in water. Underground water here has created large cavities beneath this fragile mantle. This type of terrain is known as karst, and this area is the best example of karst terrain in North America. As the bedrock continues to dissolve, the underground caves enlarge, eventually collapsing under their own weight, forming large depressions known as **sinkholes.** The thousands of sinkholes here vary in size from three meters (10 feet) to 100 meters (330 feet) across. The most accessible large sinkhole is behind the Angus Fire Tower, 150 kilometers (93 miles) west of Fort Smith.

The **Peace-Athabasca Delta** is in a remote part of this remote park and is rarely visited. Getting to the delta requires some planning because no roads access the area. The most popular visitor destination on the delta is **Sweetgrass Station,** located 12 kilometers (7.5 miles) south of the Peace River. The site is on the edge of a vast meadow that extends around the north and west shore of Lake Claire, providing a summer range for most of the park's bison. A cabin with bunks and a woodstove is available for visitors to the area at no charge, although reservations at the park information center are required. The cabin is an excellent base for exploring the meadows around Lake Claire and viewing the abundant wildlife. From Fort Smith, **Northwestern Air** (867/872-2216, www.nwal.ca), charges around $500 each way to fly two people and their gear between Fort Smith and Sweetgrass Station.

Practicalities

The **Visitor Reception Centre** (126 McDougal Rd., Fort Smith, 867/872-7900, Mon.–Fri. 9 A.M.–5 P.M. plus summer weekends 1–5 P.M.) offers trail information, a short slideshow, and an exhibit room. Another park office (780/697-3662), open similar hours, is in Fort Chipewyan.

Within the park itself, the only developed facilities are at **Pine Lake,** 60 kilometers (37 miles) south of Fort Smith. The lake has a campground ($15.70 per night) with pit toilets, covered kitchen shelters, and firewood ($6.80 per bundle). On a spit of land jutting into the lake beyond the campground is a picnic area with bug-proof shelters. The park staff presents a summer interpretive program at various locations; check the schedule at the park information center or on the campground notice board.

HAY RIVER TO YELLOWKNIFE

Yellowknife, on the north shore of the Great Slave Lake, is a long 480-kilometer (300-mile) haul from Hay River, through a monotonous boreal forest of spruce, poplar, and jack pine.

Note: Twice a year, for a few days or up to three weeks (at breakup and freeze-up, respectively, of the Mackenzie River), the road to Yellowknife is not passable (call 800/661-0750 or check online at www.gov.nt.ca for current conditions). In summer, the free ferry operates daily 6 A.M.–midnight, while in winter an ice road is constructed across the river.

Lady Evelyn Falls Territorial Park

From Enterprise, south of Hay River, Highway 1 heads northwest, coming to Lady Evelyn Falls Territorial Park after 53 kilometers (33 miles). The namesake falls, where the wide **Kakisa River** cascades off a 15-meter (50-

foot) escarpment, are easily accessible from the highway, seven kilometers (4.3 miles) down a gravel road. A short trail leads from the day-use area down to a platform overlooking the falls. The falls are part of a territorial park that has a **campground** (mid-May–mid-Sept., $17) with pit toilets, bug-proof cooking shelters, and firewood.

Fort Providence

The highway forks 85 kilometers (53 miles) from Enterprise: To the left, Highway 1 continues west to Fort Simpson, and to the right, Highway 3 heads north toward Yellowknife. Highway 3 crosses the Mackenzie River via a ferry, 24 kilometers (15 miles) from the junction. Across the river and just up the highway, a spur road leads eight kilometers (five miles) to the Slavey Dene community of Fort Providence (population 600), perched high above the river on its steep northern bank. On the riverfront through town, markers honor the roles played in the region's history by Alexander Mackenzie and the Church.

Rae-Edzo

Rae-Edzo, 214 kilometers (133 miles) north of Fort Providence, is the largest Dene community in the Northwest Territories, with a population of 1,500 Dogrib Dene. They settled around a Hudson's Bay Company post as early as 1852. In the 1960s, the government began developing a new townsite, Edzo, closer to the highway. The school at Rae was closed, and a new one opened at Edzo. Today, most of the people continue living at Rae, where the water access is better for fishing and hunting, whereas the government buildings are up on the highway at Edzo. The 10-kilometer (6.2-mile) side trip to Rae is worth taking. The resilient community is perched on a rocky outcrop jutting into **Marian Lake.** The main road through town leads to a small island, where the rocky beaches are littered with boats, fishing nets, and dogs tied up waiting for snow. Apart from the snowmobiles, the village looks much as it did 100 years ago.

NORTHWEST TERRITORIES

Yellowknife

Built on dreams, perseverance, and the ingenuity of a small group of pioneers who came in search of gold, the territorial capital of Yellowknife has grown into a modern urban center of 16,000. Its frontier-town flavor and independent spirit distinguish it from all other Canadian cities. It's the northernmost city in Canada, the *only* city in the Northwest Territories, and the only predominantly non-native community in the territories. Located on the North Arm of the Great Slave Lake, the city clings precariously to the ancient, glacial-scarred rock of the Canadian Shield. Edmonton is 1,530 kilometers (950 miles) south by road, 965 kilometers (600 miles) by air. The Arctic Circle is 440 kilometers (273 miles) north.

At first, Yellowknife looks little different from other small Canadian cities, but unique contrasts soon become apparent. Some residents write computer programs for a living, whereas others prepare caribou hides; architect-designed houses are scattered among squatters' log cabins; and the roads are seemingly always under repair, a legacy of permafrost. To the Dene, Yellowknife is known as *Som bak'e* (Place of Money).

History

Samuel Hearne dubbed the local Dene natives the Yellowknife for the copper knives they used. Miners on their way to the Klondike were the first to discover gold in the area, but they didn't rush in to stake claims because of the area's remote location and the difficulty of extracting the mineral from the hard bedrock. But as airplanes began opening up the north, the area became more attractive to gold seekers. Hundreds of claims were staked between 1934 and 1936, and a boomtown sprang up along the shore of Yellowknife Bay. After the war, growth continued, and soon the original townsite around the bay was at full capacity. A new town, just up the hill, was surveyed, and by 1947 the city center of today began taking shape. In 1967, a road was completed to the outside and the city came to rely less on air travel. The city was named the

territorial capital the same year. The last gold mine closed in 2004, but this coincided with the beginning of a diamond rush. Although these precious gems lie in the Canadian shield hundreds of kilometers north of Yellowknife, the city is the center of resource development, as well as services such as cutting and polishing, giving claim to the title "Diamond Capital of North America."

SIGHTS
◖ Prince of Wales Northern Heritage Centre

The entire history of the Northwest Territories is cataloged at this modern facility (4750 48th St., 867/873-7551, June–Aug. daily 10:30 A.M.– 5:30 P.M., the rest of the year Mon.–Fri. 10:30 A.M.–5 P.M. and Sat.–Sun. noon–5 P.M., free), within walking distance of downtown and on the shore of Frame Lake. The Feature II Gallery displays a collection of Dene, Métis, and Inuit artifacts, while the Land Speaks Gallery catalogs the arrival of European explorers, miners, and missionaries and their impact on the environment. Meanwhile, the Aviation Gallery presents a realistic display of a bush pilot and his plane, and features a wall of fame for the pilots who helped open up the north. Also here is a live hookup to the traffic controllers at Yellowknife Airport. A library stocks 6,000 historical and fiction books on the north.

Legislative Assembly of the Northwest Territories

This building on the shore of Frame Lake is the heart of territorial politics. Opened in 1993, it was designed to blend in with the surrounding landscape and made use of Northern materials. Through the front doors of a massive glass-walled facade is the Great Hall, topped by skylights and lined with the artwork of Angus Cockney. The building's centerpiece is the circular Chamber, in which the members of the legislative assembly sit facing the Speaker. Behind the Speaker stretches a massive zinc-

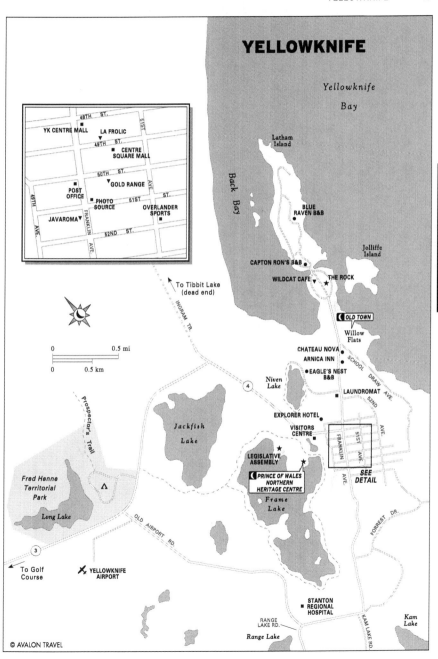

YELLOWKNIFE

Yellowknife Bay

Latham Island

Back Bay

Jolliffe Island

BLUE RAVEN B&B

CAPTON RON'S B&B

WILDCAT CAFE ★ THE ROCK

OLD TOWN

Willow Flats

To Tibbit Lake (dead end)

INGRAM TR.

CHATEAU NOVA
ARNICA INN
EAGLE'S NEST B&B

SCHOOL DRAW AVE.

Niven Lake

LAUNDROMAT

52ND AVE.

EXPLORER HOTEL

VISITORS CENTRE

Jackfish Lake

LEGISLATIVE ASSEMBLY ★

FRANKLIN

51ST AVE.

SEE DETAIL

★ PRINCE OF WALES NORTHERN HERITAGE CENTRE

Frame Lake

Prospector's Trail

Fred Henne Territorial Park

Long Lake

OLD AIRPORT RD.

FORREST DR.

To Golf Course

✈ YELLOWKNIFE AIRPORT

STANTON REGIONAL HOSPITAL

KAM LAKE RD.

Kam Lake

RANGE LAKE RD.

Range Lake

0   0.5 mi
0   0.5 km

© AVALON TRAVEL

Detail inset:

48TH ST.

YK CENTRE MALL   LA FROLIC

51ST AVE.

48TH ST.

CENTRE SQUARE MALL

50TH ST.

GOLD RANGE

POST OFFICE

PHOTO SOURCE

51ST ST.

OVERLANDER SPORTS

FRANKLIN AVE.

JAVAROMA

52ND ST.

49TH AVE.

plated mural of a Northern landscape. The building is open Mon.–Fri. 7 A.M.–6 P.M., Sat.–Sun. 10 A.M.–6 P.M. Free one-hour tours (867/669-2300) are offered June to August Mon.–Fri. at 10:30 A.M., 1:30 P.M., and 3:30 P.M. and Sunday at 1:30 P.M., the rest of the year weekdays only at 10:30 A.M. Outside you'll find Capital Area Park and a Ceremonial Circle comprising flags that represent each of the territories' 33 communities.

◖ Old Town

From the city center, Franklin Avenue (50th Ave.) descends a long, dusty hill to Yellowknife's Old Town. In the 1930s, the first log and frame buildings were erected at this site. Along the narrow streets, Quonset huts, original settlers' homes, converted buses, old boats, and tin shanties look incongruous in a Canadian capital city. Some of the most unusual housing is in **Willow Flats,** east of Franklin Avenue. **Ragged Ass Road,** named for a mine claim, has the most unusual houses, many posting signs telling the story of the building. Farther north along Franklin Avenue is an area known simply as **The Rock,** for the huge chunk of Canadian Shield that towers above the surrounding landscape. At the top of The Rock is the **Pilot's Monument,** dedicated to the bush pilots who opened up the north. At the corner of Pilots Lane and Wiley Road is **Weaver & Devore,** an old-time general store selling just about everything. Many of their larger orders have to be flown in to buyers scattered throughout the north. East of The Rock, in Yellowknife Bay, is **Jolliffe Island,** once a fuel depot but now a residential area. The homes are reached by boat or canoe in summer and by road in winter. At the north end of The Rock, a causeway, built in 1948, connects **Latham Island** to the mainland. At the south end of the island are floatplane bases, where the constant buzz of small planes taking off and landing symbolizes the north.

Ingraham Trail

Apart from Highway 3 from the south, the Ingraham Trail (Hwy. 4 East) is the only route out of the city. It then crosses the Yellowknife River and passes **Prosperous, Pontoon,** and **Prelude Lakes,** each with day-use areas and great for fishing, boating, and swimming. Continuing east, the road parallels the Cameron River within **Hidden Lake Territorial Park,** 48 kilometers (30 miles) from Yellowknife. Trails lead down to the riverbank, and waterfalls dot the park. The road ends at **Tibbit Lake,** 71 kilometers (44 miles) from Yellowknife.

Fred Henne Territorial Park

Forest-encircled **Long Lake,** opposite Yellowknife Airport, is used by visitors mainly for the excellent camping facilities, but it's also a good example of the wilderness surrounding the city. The four-kilometer (2.5-mile) round-trip **Prospector's Trail,** which begins from the campground, is a good way to experience the unique landscape. You can hike to the park from the city center along the trails around **Frame Lake.**

RECREATION
Fishing and Canoeing

The brochures of many fishing-charter operators fill the Northern Frontier Regional Visitors Centre, but Greg Robertson at **Bluefish Services** (867/873-4818, www.bluefishservices.ca) offers the widest range of fishing opportunities, including fishing for arctic grayling from local river banks, chasing northern pike out on North Arm, and trawling the deepest parts of Great Slave Lake for massive lake trout. A four-hour trip, which includes fishing, sightseeing, and a fish fry, is $110 per person. For serious anglers, full-day fishing costs $235. **Enodah Wilderness Travel** (867/873-4334, www.enodah.com) has a lodge on Trout Rock, a small island 30 kilometers (19 miles) west of Yellowknife that was once the site of a Dogrib community. A day trip including guided fishing and access by floatplane is $520 per person, and three-day fishing trips are $1,685 per person.

Overlander Sports (4909 50th St., 867/873-2474, closed Sun.) rents canoes and kayaks for $45 per day, which allows enough time to explore nearby Jolliffe Island and its surrounding waters. For those interested in longer trips, weekly rates are $200.

◖ Golfing Under the Midnight Sun

For a unique Northern experience, consider playing 18 holes at **Yellowknife Golf Club** (west of town along Hwy. 3, 867/873-4326, May–Sept.), where the "greens" are artificial grass, and to combat rock and gravel fairways, each shot must be hit from a small mat that players carry around the course. Greens fee is $36 and mat rental is $5, and you can tee off day and night in late June and early July. Aside from the unique playing conditions, facilities are similar to those at any regular golf course: a pro shop with rentals ($21), a driving range, a restaurant, and a beer cart, of course. Also look in the clubhouse for some great photos of the course's early days.

NIGHTLIFE

Entertainment at the **Gold Range Hotel** (5010 50th St., 867/873-4441), best known as the "Strange Range," is like no other in the country. Don't be put off by the unusual characters, hundreds of empty beer glasses, and bouncers with legs like tree trunks; it isn't as rowdy as it seems. If you like to mix with the locals, this is the place to do it, and you may help them claim the title for highest beer sales per capita in Canada; so far they run only second. For something a little more subdued, plan on relaxing at the **Trapline Lounge** in the Explorer Hotel (4825 49th Ave., 867/873-3531).

FESTIVALS AND EVENTS

The week closest to the longest day of the year (June 21) is the **Sumer Solstice Festival** (www.solsticefestival.ca), featuring street entertainment, celebrations of native culture, and the Canadian North Midnight Classic (this event is popular with visitors, so make reservations in advance (867/873-4326, www.yellowknifegolf. com). **Folk on the Rocks** (867/920-7806, www. folkontherocks.com), held during the middle

weekend of July, takes place on the shore of Long Lake and attracts Northern and Southern performers of folk, reggae, and Inuit music. A weekend ticket is $100. On the other side of the calendar, the **Caribou Carnival** (www.cariboucarnival.net) began more than 50 years ago among locals as a test of outdoor skills. It still tests the locals, who compete in a variety of themed events, but there's also a children's tent, native displays, live music, pancake breakfasts, and delicacies such as caribou cake for visitors to try. The action takes place throughout the city on the last weekend in March.

ACCOMMODATIONS AND CAMPING
$50-100

The only accommodations with rooms for less than $100 are bed-and-breakfasts. Ask at the Visitors Centre for a current list of B&Bs, or contact **Captain Ron's** (8 Lessard Dr., 867/873-3746, $85 s, $95 d), overlooking the floatplane base. It has four guest rooms, a sundeck, a library, and a guest lounge.

$100-200

◖ **Eagle's Nest B&B** (222 Niven Dr., 867/920-2688, www.ykeaglesnest.ca, $100 s, $110 d) is a modern home in a new housing estate, and a 10-minute walk from both downtown and Old Town. Three of the four smallish guest rooms share a bathroom, but all have a clean, modern outlook, with hardwood floors and comfortable beds. Amenities include a living room, business center, den, private balconies, and a kitchen open for guest use. Rates include a light breakfast.

Yellowknife's least expensive motel is the **Arnica Inn** (4115 Franklin Ave., 867/873-8511, www.arnicainn.ca, $149–169 s or d), halfway between downtown and Old Town. Rooms are in reasonable shape and come with wireless Internet. The small in-house café is inexpensive and open daily for breakfast and lunch.

Chateau Nova (4401 50th Ave., 867/873-9700 or 877/839-1236, www.chateaunova. com, $179–219 s or d) is the rather grand name of a newish hotel a few blocks from downtown on the way to Old Town. Rooms are modern and come with niceties such as bathrobes and a writing desk. Other amenities include free airport shuttles, a small fitness room with a big hot tub, a business center with Internet access, spa services, and a restaurant with the best pizza in town.

$200-250

With 187 rooms, the **(Explorer Hotel** (4825 49th Ave., 867/873-3531 or 800/661-0892, www. explorerhotel.ca, $220–232 s or d) is Yellowknife's largest accommodation. It also has the nicest rooms, with modern conveniences such as coffeemakers, hairdryers, and free wireless Internet, as well as big city extras such as room service and free airport shuttles. It also has a restaurant, lounge, fitness room, and gift shop.

Camping

The city's only campground is at **Fred Henne Territorial Park** (867/920-2472, $17–21), across from the airport and a one-hour walk from downtown. Amenities include bug-proof cooking shelters, woodstoves, showers, and some powered sites. Along the Ingraham Trail, at Reid Lake, and at Prelude Lake Territorial Parks are primitive campgrounds. All three are open mid-May–mid-September and online reservations can be made at www.campingnwt.ca.

FOOD

Yellowknife has a decent selection of restaurants, as well as all the usual fast-food choices, and city-style coffee at places like **Javaroma** (5201 50th Ave., 867/669-0725). Head to **Northern Fancy Meats** (314 Woolgar Ave., 867/873-8767, Mon.–Sat. 9 A.M.–6 P.M.) for Northern game meat and in-house sausages and jerky.

Downtown

Of the many hotel dining rooms, none is better than **Traders Grill** (Explorer Hotel, 4825 49th Ave., 867/873-3531, Mon.–Fri 7 A.M.–9 P.M., Sat.–Sun. 8 A.M.–9 P.M., $22–38), a stylish space with professional service and a wide-ranging menu that includes a few local seafood choices (crumbed turbot, seafood chowder, and baked arctic char). Cooked breakfasts top out at $15 for eggs Benedict made with smoked arctic char.

Le Frolic (5019 49th St., 867/669-9852, $17–35) is the downstairs half of a French restaurant combo (L'Heritage, upstairs, is more formal and expensive) that presents game like arctic char, musk ox, and caribou with French flair. With the bison burger at $17, you don't need to spend a fortune, but the wild-game fondue (deer, caribou, and bison) with seasoned game broth is hard to pass up.

Old Town

Head down the hill from the city center to enjoy Northern cuisine and typically hospitable Northern atmosphere at any of the following restaurants. The **(Wildcat Café** (3904 Wiley Rd., 867/873-8850, June–Aug. Mon.–Sat. 7:30 A.M.–9 P.M. and Sun. 10 A.M.–9 P.M., $19–28) has been famous since it was opened by Willy Wiley and Smoky Stout in 1937, becoming the first place in Yellowknife to sell ice cream. The café closed its doors in 1959 but reopened with some remodeling in 1977. The distinctive Northern feel hasn't been lost—log walls, wooden tables, a sloping floor, and a congenial atmosphere are part of the charm. It only has a few tables and is perpetually full, so chances are you'll end up sharing a table. The blackboard menu changes daily but features dishes such as lake trout, whitefish, and musk ox.

INFORMATION

The **Northern Frontier Regional Visitors Centre** (4807 49th St., 867/873-4262 or 877/881-4261, www.northernfrontier.com, June–Aug. daily 8:30 A.M.–6 P.M., the rest of the year Mon.–Fri. 8:30 A.M.–5:30 P.M., Sat.–Sun. noon–4 P.M.) overlooks Frame Lake. It's stocked with brochures on everything you'll need to know about Yellowknife, historic photographs, and interesting displays.

Libraries and Bookstores

On the second floor of Centre Square Mall is

Yellowknife Public Library (5022 49th St., 867/920-5642, Mon.–Thurs. 10 A.M.–9 P.M., Fri.–Sat. 10 A.M.–6 P.M.). Although small, it has newspapers from throughout Canada, lots of literature on the north, and public Internet access. **Yellowknife Book Cellar** (Panda II Mall, 867/920-2220, www.yellowknifebooks. com) has a wide selection of Northern and Canadian literature. In addition to walk-in customers, they serve Northerners looking for specialty titles and outsiders looking for local literature.

SERVICES

The post office is at 4902 50th Street. Public Internet access is free at the library or head to **Frostbyte Café** (5110 50th Ave., 867/669-8840). Wash clothes at the **Arctic Laundromat** (4310 Franklin Ave., daily 8:30 A.M.–11 P.M.). **Yellowknife Foto Source** (5005 Franklin Ave., 867/873-2196) entered the digital age as quickly as any Southern photo shop. Stop by for parts, service, or to download digital files to print.

Stanton Regional Hospital (867/920-4111) is on Old Airport Road at Range Lake Road. For the **RCMP,** call 867/669-5100.

GETTING THERE

Yellowknife Airport, five kilometers (3.1 miles) west of the city along Highway 3, is the hub of air travel in the Northwest Territories.

It's open daily 24 hours, has an inexpensive café (5:30 A.M.–10 P.M.), a bar, lockers, and rental car desks. **First Air** (867/669-8500 or 800/267-1247) uses Yellowknife as its western hub, with flights arriving and departing daily from Edmonton, Inuvik, and many Nunavut communities. Other airlines flying in and out of the capital include **Canadian North** (867/873-4484 or 800/661-1505), and **Northwestern Air** (867/872-2216 or 877/872-2216).

Frontier Coachlines (113 Kamlake Rd., 867/873-4892) offers bus service five times weekly from Hay River to Yellowknife, with connections from there to Greyhound's other Canadian services.

GETTING AROUND

Yellowknife Transit (867/873-4693, adult $2.50, senior and child $1.50 per sector) operates along three routes, including out to the campground and airport, Monday–Friday and with a limited Saturday service. Cab companies are **City Cab** (867/873-4444) and **Sunshine Taxi** (867/873-4414). Rental-car agencies include **Budget** (867/920-9209), **Hertz** (867/766-3838), and **National** (867/873-3424). Rates start at $60 per day and $360 per week for a small car. Generally no mileage allowance is given on daily rentals, but you get 250 kilometers included with weekly rentals.

Nahanni Country and the Mackenzie Valley

The Dene word for "spirit," Nahanni Country extends west from where the main highway north to Yellowknife crosses the Mackenzie River to the utter wilderness of the Mackenzie Mountains. The two main towns of Fort Simpson and Fort Liard are jumping-off points for the real adventure—rafting down the South Nahanni River through Nahanni National Park.

WEST TO FORT SIMPSON

From the Yellowknife junction, the Mackenzie Highway continues west through a typical northern boreal forest, reaching the largest town in the region, Fort Simpson, after 268 kilometers (166 miles). The road is unpaved but well maintained.

Sambaa Deh Falls Territorial Park

Approximately 136 kilometers (84 miles) from the turn-off at Highway 3, the Mackenzie Highway reaches Sambaa Deh Falls on the Trout River. The falls are directly downstream from the road bridge and are easily accessible from the day-use area, on the other side of the road. Here, the river is forced through a narrow gorge, exploding into the deep pond below. A one-kilometer (0.6-mile) trail upstream leads to a fossil-filled limestone outcrop. The park has camping (showers, bug-proof cooking shelters, and well-maintained sites for $17 per night) and a **Visitors Centre** (daily 8 A.M.–8 P.M. mid-May–mid-Sept.) with a fossil display and TV room where nature videos are shown.

FORT SIMPSON

Best known as an access point for Nahanni National Park, the town of Fort Simpson (population 1,200) is at the confluence of two major rivers—the Liard and Mackenzie—with ferry crossing (daily 8 A.M.–11:45 P.M. late May–late Oct., free) required to reach town from the Mackenzie Highway. Throughout summer, the town is a hive of activity, with a constant buzz of floatplanes taking off to remote fly-in fishing lakes and hunt camps, groups of Gore-Tex–clad adventurers from around the world checking their equipment before heading off for the adventure of a lifetime down the South Nahanni River, and the occasional canoe-load of paddlers stopping in on their way to the Arctic Ocean.

Sights and Recreation

The main street through Fort Simpson is typical of Northern towns, with all the usual services, a couple of motels, and lots of modular buildings. The most interesting sights are one block east on Mackenzie Drive, running alongside the Mackenzie River. This was the main street before the highway was completed and businesses moved closer to it. At the south end, a beached stern-wheeler on the riverbank soon comes into view. Built in 1920, this boat was one of many that plied the Mackenzie River. Also here is a small monument noting the importance of the river in the town's history. Across the road is **Fort Simpson Heritage Park,** the site of the original Hudson's Bay Company post (the only original building remaining is the company's outhouse). Here you find a restored home used for various cultural

ALBERT FAILLE

Each spring from 1916-1961, Albert Faille left Fort Simpson by scow in a feverish, determined quest for the elusive Nahanni gold. Some said it was sheer lunacy, others a waste of time. But his relentless obsession and exploits against insurmountable odds created the Faille legend, which has become synonymous with the Nahanni.

Of Swiss descent, Faille was born in Minnesota. He was one of the earliest men to tackle the river alone, and at the time, the first to winter there in seven years. He built a cabin at the mouth of the Flat River, but it was at Murder Creek, upstream from the cabin, that Faille believed his fortune in gold lay. At times he'd be given up for dead, and rumors and tales would begin to unfold – but then he would turn up at Fort Simpson for supplies. He spent most winters in a small cabin that still stands today, overlooking the Mackenzie River in Fort Simpson. He died there in 1974. His scows still lie out front, ready for breakup and another attempt for the elusive key to finding gold. His final trip is documented by a 1961 National Film Board production that can be seen in the Fort Simpson and Blackstone visitors centers.

gatherings. Continuing farther along the river, you pass plaques noting the historic importance of various structures, including the cabin of Nahanni legend **Albert Faille,** who wintered here between his gold-seeking trips. Peering through the windows and marveling at the wooden scows laying in the yard gives you some insight into the life of this amazing man, particularly if you've watched the National Film Board documentary about him shown at the Visitors Centre.

Many local lakes have great fishing for northern pike, pickerel, lake trout, and arctic grayling, but are only accessible by air. **Simpson Air** (867/695-2505, www.simpsonair.ca) flies to Little Doctor Lake, where they operate a lodge, as well as **McGill Lake** and **Mustard Lake.**

Accommodations and Food

Along the road into town is 🄲 **Bannockland B&B** (867/695-3337, $155–175 s or d). Rates for the five rooms include a cooked breakfast and airport transfers. Rooms in both of Fort Simpson's hotels are little more than basic and both charge from $120 s, $140 d. They are the **Maroda Motel** (867/695-2602), where some rooms have kitchenettes, and the **Nahanni Inn** (867/695-2201), which has a coffee shop (open daily at 8 a.m.) and dining room.

On the road to the Papal Grounds is **Fort Simpson Territorial Park** (mid-May–mid-Sept., $17), where 32 sites (four with power hookups) provide ample privacy. Showers and a large supply of firewood are available.

Information and Services

At the south entrance to town is the excellent **Fort Simpson Visitor Centre** (867/695-3182, www.fortsimpson.com, mid-May–mid-Sept. daily 9 a.m.–8 p.m.), which contains a re-creation of the original Hudson's Bay Company post and some interesting historical displays. Don't miss the 1961 National Film Board documentary on Nahanni legend Albert Faille, which is shown, along with others, in the theater. Diagonally opposite the Visitors Centre is the **Tourist Service Centre,** with coin showers, a car wash, and a laundry. The library (Antoine Dr.) has public Internet access.

LIARD HIGHWAY

From the Mackenzie Highway, southeast of Fort Simpson, to Fort Nelson (British Columbia) is 394 kilometers (245 miles) of relatively straight road through a boreal forest of spruce, aspen, and poplar. Wildlife along this route is abundant; chances are you'll see moose and black bears, especially at dawn and dusk. The only services are at Fort Liard.

Blackstone Territorial Park

A little more than 100 kilometers (62 miles) from the Mackenzie Highway, where the Blackstone River drains into the Liard River, a small territorial park has been established at a site known as **Blackstone Landing.** Inside the park visitors center (daily 8 a.m.–8 p.m. mid-May–mid-Sept.) are some interesting displays on the area's history and a good selection of locally made documentaries to watch. The center is the starting point for a short trail that leads to a trapper's cabin. The park's campground ($21) has flush toilets, showers, and two bug-proof, woodstove-equipped cooking shelters. Black bears are common, so keep your food securely stored.

FORT LIARD

Best known as the "Tropics of the North" for its warm microclimate (many locals maintain vegetable gardens), this town of 400 is set among a lush forest of poplar and birch on the banks of the Liard River. The area has been settled since 1807, when the North West Company established where the Petitot River drains into the Liard. Until the 1960s, most of the Dene inhabitants spent winter away from Fort Liard, and modern development didn't begin until the highway opened to Fort Nelson. Traditional lifestyles are still important to residents, nearly all of whom spend time trapping, hunting, fishing, and making clothing and crafts.

Birchbark Baskets

The women of Fort Liard are famous for these baskets, made for storing food, collecting berries, carrying supplies, or even boiling water. Birch is abundant in the area and has a remarkably pliable nature, ideal for bending and sewing. The bark contains a natural wax, making it not only rot-resistant but also waterproof. Baskets are still made in the long, tedious process handed down from generation to generation. They are sewn together with specially prepared roots and decorated with porcupine quills. Available from the small gift store on Fort Liard's main street (or in Fort Simpson and Hay River), they make a wonderfully authentic Northern souvenir.

Practicalities

The small but well-maintained **Hay Lake**

Campground has pit toilets, firewood, and drinking water. It's along the Fort Liard access road. Accommodations above the **Liard Valley General Store** (867/770-4441, $125 s, $150 d) sleep 24 in 12 basic rooms. Back out on the highway is the only gas station (7 A.M.–11 P.M.) between Fort Simpson and Fort Nelson.

◖ NAHANNI NATIONAL PARK

One of the most spectacular, wildest, and purest stretches of white water in the world is the **South Nahanni River.** Protecting a 300-kilometer (186-mile) stretch of this remote river is 4,766-square-kilometer (1,234-square-mile) Nahanni National Park. This roadless park is a vast wilderness inhabited only by bears, mountain goats, Dall sheep, caribou, moose, and wolves.

Accessible only by air, the best way to really experience the park is on a raft or canoe trip down the South Nahanni River, but many visitors just fly in for the day. However you decide to visit the park, the adventure will remain with you for the rest of your life. But with names on the map like Headless Creek, Deadmen Valley, Hell's Gate, Funeral Range, Devils Kitchen, Broken Skull River, and Death Canyon, you'd better tell someone where you're going before heading out.

History

Slavey Dene, who lived on the lowlands along the Mackenzie and Liard Rivers, feared a mysterious group of natives living high in the Mackenzie Mountains, calling them the *Nahanni* (People Who Live Far Away). The first white men to travel up the South Nahanni River were fur trappers and missionaries, followed by men lured by tales of gold. In 1905, Willie and Frank McLeod began prospecting tributaries of the Flat River in search of an elusive mother lode. Three years later, their headless bodies were discovered at the mouth of what is now known as Headless Creek; for many years thereafter, the entire valley was called Deadmen Valley. Very quickly, stories of gold mines, murder, lush tropical valleys, and a tribe of Indians dominated by a white woman became rampant. These stories did nothing but lure other prospecting adventurers to the valley—Jorgenson, Shebbach, Field, Faille, Sibbeston, Kraus, and Patterson. Many died mysteriously: Jorgenson's skeleton was found outside his cabin, his precious rifle gone; Shebbach died of starvation at the mouth of Caribou Creek; the body of Phil Powers was discovered in his burned-out cabin; Angus Hall just plain disappeared.

The Land

The headwaters of the **South Nahanni River** are high in **Mackenzie Mountains,** which form the remote border between the Northwest Territories and the Yukon. Flowing in a roughly southeasterly direction for 540 kilometers (336 miles) it drains into the Liard River, a major tributary of the Mackenzie River. The South Nahanni, cut deeply into the mountains, is known as an "antecedent;" that is, it preceded the mountains. It once meandered through a wide-open plain. As uplift in the earth's surface occurred, the river cut down through the rising rock strata and created the deep, meandering canyons present today.

The starting point for many river trips and the destination of most day trippers is **Virginia Falls;** at 92 meters (300 feet) they are twice as high as Niagara Falls. Over many thousands of years, erosion has forced the falls upstream, creating a canyon system with walls over one kilometer (0.6 miles) high immediately downstream of the falls.

Running the South Nahanni with an Outfitter

For most people, whether experienced or first-time canoeists, the advantages of a trip down the South Nahanni River with a licensed outfitter far outweigh the disadvantages.

The two outfitters I recommend are **Nahanni River Adventures** (867/668-3180 or 800/297-6927, www.nahanni.com) and **Nahanni Wilderness Adventures** (403/678-3374 or 888/897-5223, www.nahanniwild.com). Each offers trips of varying lengths—8–12 days from Virginia Falls, two weeks from

Rabbitkettle Lake, or up to three weeks from Moose Ponds. Crafts used are rafts, two-person canoes, or longer voyageur-type canoes. Trips start at $3,900 for an eight-day float. The best way to get a feeling for which trip suits your needs and interests is by talking to the outfitters (they all love "their" river, so getting them to talk is no problem). Guided trips operate mid-June–early September, and many dates fill up fast. The staging area for both outfitters is the north end of the old airstrip in downtown Fort Simpson.

Your Own White-Water Expedition

Experienced white-water enthusiasts planning their own trip down the Nahanni have four main components to organize: permits and fees, transportation into the park, transportation down the river, and supplies. The best place to start planning your trip is the Parks Canada website (www.pc.gc.ca/nahanni), where you can download reservation forms and pay the park use fee ($147.20 per person). Only 12 non-guided visitors are allowed to start down the river each day, so reservations are an absolute necessity. Most expeditions begin with a floatplane trip to Virginia Falls and end outside of the park, where the Liard River flows alongside the Liard Highway. The charter cost from Fort Simpson to Virginia Falls for two people, one canoe, and 500 pounds of gear, is around $1,200. This is just an example—if there are four of you, you would travel in a bigger plane (a Beaver) and the cost would run around $2,000. For detailed quotes contact **Simpson Air** (867/695-2505, www.simpsonair.ca) or **Wolverine Air** (867/695-2263, www.wolverineair.com). These are the same two companies used by commercial guides, so they're flying into the park all the time. A few years ago, I picked up a guy who'd just come down the river and was hitchhiking back to Watson Lake from Blackstone Landing. He'd started at Moose Ponds, which is closer to Watson Lake (Yukon) than any Northwest Territories community; therefore chartering a plane from Watson Lake costs less, but it seemed an inconvenient way to save a couple hundred bucks. If you need a canoe or other equipment, contact the floatplane companies or the commercial outfitters for rentals.

Flightseeing

Calling a flightseeing trip into Nahanni "awe-inspiring" doesn't do it justice—it is simply one of the most memorable flights I have ever taken. Getting into the park for just the day is problematic but well worth the effort and cost. Typically, charter operators use a floatplane to fly from Fort Simpson to Virginia Falls, with up to two hours spent at the falls, enough time to walk the 1.3-kilometer (0.8-mile) portage to the base of the falls. If you have three or more people in your group, there are no problems; just call each operator for the best quote (or get the staff at Fort Simpson Visitor Centre to do it for you) and expect to pay around $500 per person for a four- to five-hour trip. Groups of less than three have the choice of chartering an entire plane (from approximately $1,400) or waiting around for other interested parties to turn up. Each of the air charter companies can tailor flights to suit your needs. By waiting around until the plane is full, or by booking in advance, you have a better chance of keeping the cost down. Fort Simpson operators are the following: **Simpson Air** (867/695-2505) or **Wolverine Air** (867/695-2263).

Information

The outfitters on the river are experts in their own right and can answer many of your questions long before you arrive. For specific information on the park, check the website (www.pc.gc.ca/nahanni) or contact **Park Headquarters** in Fort Simpson (867/695-3151). The **Fort Simpson Visitor Centre** (867/695-3182, mid-May–mid-Sept. 9 A.M.–8 P.M.) has park displays as well as relevant videos and books for visitor use.

TOWNS ALONG THE MACKENZIE RIVER

In 1789, Alexander Mackenzie became the first European to travel the river that now bears his name. After his reports of rich fur resources

NORTHWEST TERRITORIES

reached the outside, the North West Company established fur-trading posts along the river. The Dene, who were originally nomadic, settled at the trading posts, forming small communities that still exist today. The only road into the region begins at Fort Simpson and extends north to Wrigley.

Wrigley

The road between Fort Simpson and Wrigley traverses thick boreal forest, breaking only for a short ferry trip at **Ndulee** (daily 9–11 A.M. and 2–8 P.M.), 84 kilometers (52 miles) out of Fort Simpson.

Most of the community's 160 residents are Slavey Dene who live a semi-traditional lifestyle. Across the Yukon River from the village is **Roche qui-Trempe-à -L'eau** (The Rock that Plunges into the Water), an isolated hill that has been eroded away by the river on one side, creating a sheer cliff that drops 400 meters (1,300 feet) into the water below.

The **Petanea Hotel** (867/581-3102, www. wrigleyhotel.com) is in a modular building that holds five guest rooms. Rates are $240 per person per day with three meals. The hotel also has a small coffee shop and a dining room that opens in the evening. Enquire here about boat rentals and tours.

Norman Wells

Oil is the lifeblood of Norman Wells (population 800), which lies along the Mackenzie River halfway between Fort Simpson and Inuvik. Unlike other settlements along the Mackenzie River, Norman Wells did not originate as a trading post but owes its existence to oil. Imperial Oil produces 10 million barrels annually from field tapped by over 150 wells (the company's largest source of conventional crude oil), shipping to market by pipeline. The infrastructure is unique in that it comprises man-made islands in the middle of the Mackenzie River, directly offshore from town, allowing oil extraction to continue throughout breakup and freeze-up of the river.

The center of town, a 20-minute walk from the airport, is a semicircle of semipermanent buildings around a dusty parking lot. Here you'll find the **Yamouri Inn** (867/587-2744, $130 s, $140 d), which has rooms, a dimly lit cocktail lounge, a coffee shop, and a restaurant. Closer to the airport is the **Mackenzie Valley Hotel** (867/587-2511, www.mackenzievalleyhotel.com, $130 s, $160 d). The 34 rooms are cheerfully painted and each comes with a TV and phone.

Norman Wells has an impressive three-story airport complete with an observation deck and revolving baggage claim—not bad for a town of 800 people. It is a one-kilometer (0.6-mile) walk into town. **North-Wright Airways** (867/587-2333, www.north-wrightairways. com) has daily flights from Yellowknife to Norman Wells, as well as from Norman Wells to all Mackenzie River communities.

Canol Heritage Trail

The large U.S. military force present in Alaska during World War II needed oil to fuel aircraft and ships, which were in place for expected Japanese attacks. The strategically located Norman Wells oil fields were chosen as a source of crude oil, with little regard for the engineering feat needed to build a pipeline over the Mackenzie Mountains. To this day, it remains one of the largest projects ever undertaken in northern Canada. More than $300 million was spent between 1942 and 1945, employing 30,000 people who laid 2,650 kilometers (1,650 miles) of four- and six-inch pipeline and built a road over some of North America's most isolated and impenetrable mountain ranges. It was abandoned less than a year after completion. Today, the roadbed remains—strewn with structures, trucks, and equipment used in the project's construction—and is considered by many to be one of the world's great wilderness hikes. It follows the original route for 372 kilometers (231 miles), from the Mackenzie River across from Norman Wells to the Yukon border. Following the road causes little problem, but the logistics of getting to the beginning of the trail, arranging food drops, crossing rivers (most bridges have been washed out), and returning to Norman

Wells require much planning. Rick Muyres of **Mountain River Outfitters** (867/587-2697, www.mountainriver.nt.ca) can provide transportation and logistical support.

Tulita

This small Slavey Dene community (population 300) is south of Norman Wells, where the Great Bear River drains into the Mackenzie River. This strategic location has made it a transportation hub since the days of Sir John Franklin. An Anglican church, built of squared logs and dating to the 1860s, sits on the riverbank, beside the Hudson's Bay Company post. Many houses have colorful tepees in their yards, which are used for drying and smoking fish, standing in stark contrast to a modern school building.

The **Two Rivers Hotel** (867/588-3320, $169 s, $219 d) has eight rooms with single and double beds, all with a shared bathroom and kitchen. Meals can also be arranged in the dining room. If you're interested in a boat trip chasing arctic grayling in the Great Bear River or to the **Smoking Hills,** where an exposed seam of coal burns permanently, make enquires at the hotel.

Great Bear Lake

East of the Mackenzie River, Great Bear Lake is one of the world's best freshwater fishing lakes, and it has the records to prove it. This lake holds world records for *all* line classes of lake trout and arctic grayling; the overall world record trout weighed in at a whopping 32.5 kilograms (72 pounds) and measured more than one meter (three feet). The lake also holds world records for most classes of arctic grayling, including the overall record.

Around the lake are small fishing lodges offering all-inclusive packages, including Great Bear Lake Lodge operated by **Plummer's Arctic Lodges** (204/774-5775 or 800/665-0240, www.canadianarcticfishing.com). Accommodations, all meals, guides, professionally equipped boats, and round-trip air charters from Winnipeg or Edmonton are included in the package; US$4,600 for seven days.

Formerly known as Fort Franklin, **Déline** (meaning "flowing water") is the only community on the lake. In 1825, Sir John Franklin wintered at the trading post here before setting off on one of his many expeditions in search of the Northwest Passage. Today, the Slavey Dene of Déline live a traditional lifestyle, trapping, fishing, and making crafts including moccasins for which they are well known. The tepee-shaped church is worth visiting, and the hike along the shore of Great Bear Lake offers rewarding vistas and passes several historic sites. Right in town, **Grey Goose Lodge** (867/589-5500, www.greygooselodge.ca, $185 pp including breakfast) is a modern accommodation with 12 guest rooms, canoe and motorboat rentals, and fishing charters.

Fort Good Hope

Overlooking the Mackenzie River and flanked by boreal forest, this Slavey Dene community of 550 is on the east bank of the Mackenzie River, 190 kilometers (118 miles) downstream of Norman Wells and just south of the Arctic Circle. A trading post was established here in 1805 by the North West Company, but the oldest building in town is the 1860 **Our Lady of Good Hope Church,** which has been declared a National Historic Site. The church's interior, decorated in ornate panels and friezes painted by an early missionary, Father Emile Petitot, depicts aspects of his travels and life in the north.

One of the highlights of a trip to Fort Good Hope is visiting **The Ramparts,** where 200-meter-high (660-foot) cliffs force the Mackenzie River through a 500-meter-wide (1,640-foot) canyon. Although the cliffs continue for many kilometers, the most spectacular section is upstream of town and can be reached on foot or by boat. Arrange boat rentals and tours through the **Ramparts Hotel** (867/598-2500, $165 pp). Overlooking the river, this hotel has a restaurant with a simple menu (entrées $21–32).

Colville Lake

This community of 50 North Slavey Dene,

just north of the Arctic Circle on the southeast shore of Colville Lake, was established in 1962 when a Roman Catholic mission was built. It is the territories' only community built entirely from logs. The largest building is the church, which supports a bell weighing 454 kilograms (1,000 pounds). The mission was built by Father Bern Will Brown, who has now left the church and is one of the north's most respected artists. His paintings, which depict the lifestyle of Northerners, are in demand across North America. Brown is also the host at **Colville Lake Lodge** (867/709-2500), which combines log cabin accommodation with excellent fishing for lake trout, arctic grayling, northern pike, whitefish, and inconnu, with a small museum highlighting life in the north. The lodge also has an art gallery, boat and canoe rentals, and common kitchen facilities.

Western Arctic

The northwestern corner of the Northwest Territories, where the Mackenzie River drains into the Arctic Ocean, is linked to the outside world by the Dempster Highway, the continent's northernmost public road. The region, which is entirely above the Arctic Circle, encompasses the Mackenzie River valley and the vast barrens flanking the Arctic Ocean.

INUVIK

You must see Inuvik (population 3,300) with your own eyes to believe it, and then you may still doubt what you see: brightly painted houses on stilts, a monstrous church shaped like an igloo, metal tunnels snaking through town, and a main street where businesses have names such as Eskimo Inn, 60 Below Construction, and Polar TV. Inuvik (Place of Man, in Inuvialuktun) is obviously a planned community, transformed from some architect's drafting board into full-blown reality high above the Arctic Circle. All aspects have been scientifically planned, right down to the foundations—all structures sit on piles of rock, ensuring stability in the permafrost and preventing heat from turning the ground into sludge.

Inuvik marks the end of the Dempster Highway, as far north as you can drive on a public road in North America, which is reason enough for many visitors to make the trek to town. If you come up from Calgary, you will have driven 3,560 kilometers (2,210 miles),

from Seattle 4,030 kilometers (2,500 miles), from Los Angeles 6,100 kilometers (3,790 miles), or from New York 7,600 kilometers (4,720 miles).

Sights

It's easy to spend a whole day walking around town, checking out the unique considerations involved in living above the Arctic Circle. *Utilidors,* for example, snake around town, linking businesses and houses and passing right through the middle of the schoolyard. These conduits contain water, heat, and sewerage pipelines and are raised above the ground to prevent problems associated with permafrost. Inuvik's most famous landmark is **Our Lady of Victory Church,** commonly known as the **Igloo Church** (174 Mackenzie Rd., 867/777-2236) for its distinctive shape. The church, on Mackenzie Road, is not always open; ask at the rectory for permission to enter. The interior is decorated with a series of paintings by Inuvialuit artist Mona Thrasher, depicting various religious scenes. A few blocks to the east is the **Aurora Research Institute** (191 Mackenzie Rd., 867/777-3298, Mon.–Fri. 9 A.M.–5 P.M.), one of three support facilities for scientific projects throughout the Northwest Territories. West along Mackenzie Road is **Ingamo Hall,** a three-story structure built with more than 1,000 logs. The best views of the delta are, naturally, from the air, but the next best thing is to climb the 20-meter (66-foot)

Our Lady of Victory Church, commonly known as the Igloo Church

observation tower in **Jak Territorial Park,** six kilometers (3.7 miles) south of downtown.

Tours

It seems that everyone who visits Inuvik takes at least one tour, whether it's around town, on the delta, or to an outlying community. **Arctic Nature Tours** (beside the igloo church on Mackenzie Rd., 867/777-3300, www.arctic-naturetours.com) offers an extensive variety of tours June–early September; those that require flying include transportation from town out to the airport. The town tour ($45) lasts approximately two hours, taking in all the sights. Another popular excursion is Mackenzie Delta Legends Tour to the camp of an Inuvialuit elder ($160), where tea and bannock is served. In addition to Tuktoyaktuk tours, the company has trips to remote **Herschel Island,** located in the Beaufort Sea. The island was a major whaling station during the early 1900s, but today only ruins remain. This trip is especially good for bird-watchers because more than 70 avian species have been recorded on the island. The flight to the island passes **Ivvavik National Park** in the northern Yukon, providing opportunities to see musk oxen, caribou, and grizzly bears. A two-hour stay on the island costs $425 per person, including the 90-minute (one-way) flight. Overnight stays begin at $805 per person.

Festivals and Events

Summer Solstice in June is celebrated by **Midnight Madness,** although because the sun doesn't set for a month, the actual date of the festival is of little importance. Celebrations on the weekend closest to the solstice (June 21) include traditional music and dancing and a feast of lobster imported from the east coast for the occasion. The **Great Northern Arts Festival** (www.gnaf.org), held during the third week of July, features carving demonstrations, musical performances such as Inuit drumming, displays, and sales of Northern art.

Accommodations and Camping

A few locals run bed-and-breakfasts, which are

relatively inexpensive and a friendly alternative to the impersonal hotels. Accommodations at the centrally located **☾ Polar B&B** (75 Mackenzie Rd., 867/777-2198, $105 s, $115 d) are comfortable, with a shared bathroom, kitchen, laundry, and lounge with television. Rates include a self-serve breakfast. One block farther down the hill is **Robertson's B&B** (41 Mackenzie Rd., 867/777-3111, June–Sept., $90 s, $100 d). This place has a large deck with great view of the delta. The two guest rooms share a single bathroom, but the price is right.

Inuvik's two downtown motels are owned by the Mackenzie Delta Hotel Group (www.mackenziedeltahotel.com), a native co-operative. Each has a coffee shop, a restaurant, and basic rooms with private baths. They are the uninspiring **Eskimo Inn** (133 Mackenzie Rd., 867/777-2801, $119–149 s, $129–159 d), with some rooms designated as nonsmoking, and the **Mackenzie Hotel** (185 Mackenzie Rd., 867/777-2861, $189 s, $204 d), with air-conditioning and in-room Internet access. On the way to the airport and the pick of the town's

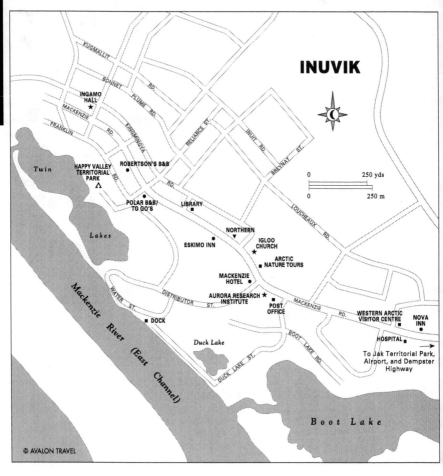

motels for room quality, is the **Nova Inn** (288 Mackenzie Rd., 867/777-2647 or 866/374-6682, www.novainninuvik.com, from $89 s, $129 d), which offers 42 comfortable rooms, each with Internet access, work desk, coffeemaker, and a fridge.

Happy Valley Territorial Park (867/777-3652, June–Aug., unserviced sites $18, powered sites $21) is on a bluff overlooking the delta, yet one block from the main street. It has 20 private, unserviced sites and a gravel parking area for RVs and trailers that need power. Amenities include flush toilets, showers, and firewood. Outside of town toward the airport is the **Jak Territorial Park** (June–Aug., unserviced sites $18, powered sites $21), with similar facilities, as well as an observation tower with river views.

Food

The thing to do this far north is to sample local fare such as musk ox, caribou, and arctic char. The least expensive way to do this is at **To Go's** (71 Mackenzie Rd., 867/777-3030), which has a few tables and a take-out menu. Caribou burgers and musk ox burgers ($8.50) are the same price as regular hamburgers but cheaper than mushroom burgers. Pizza starts at $16; extras such as musk ox are $3.50, and the Northern Pizza—with the works—is $25.

Tonimoes (Mackenzie Hotel, 185 Mackenzie Rd., 867/777-2861, Tues.–Sat. 6–10 p.m., Sunday for brunch) serves a good selection of Northern cuisine (starting at $17.95 for a caribou burger).

Information and Services

The **Western Arctic Visitor Centre** (867/777-4727, www.inuvik.ca, daily 9 a.m.–8 p.m. mid-May–mid-Sept.) is at the entrance to town, a 10-minute walk from downtown. This modern facility features displays on the people of the north, details on each of the western Arctic communities, and all the usual tour information. Out back, a trail leads through a re-creation of an Inuvialuit whaling camp and a Gwich'in fishing camp. **Inuvik Centennial Library** (100 Mackenzie Rd., 867/777-

8620, Mon.–Thurs. 10 a.m.–9 p.m., Fri. 10 a.m.–6 p.m., Sat.–Sun. 1–5 p.m.) has a fairly extensive collection of Northern books and literature, as well as free public Internet access.

The **post office** is at 817 Mackenzie Road. **Inuvik Regional Hospital** (867/777-8000) is at the east end of town.

Getting There and Around

Mike Zubko Airport, 12 kilometers (7.5 miles) south of town, is the hub of air transport in the western Arctic. A cab between the airport and downtown is $35 for one or two passengers. From Calgary and Edmonton, **First Air** (867/669-8500 or 800/267-1247) and **Canadian North** (867/873-4484 or 800/661-1505) fly to Inuvik via Yellowknife. Heading north, sit on the left side of the plane for views of the Mackenzie Mountains. The local airline, with scheduled flights to communities throughout the western Arctic, is **Aklak Air** (867/777-3777, www.aklakair.ca).

For a cab, call **United Taxi** (867/777-5050). The cabs don't have meters because fares are set: $10 anywhere around town, $45 to the airport, and $460 to Tuktoyaktuk on the winter road.

AKLAVIK

Theoretically, this community in the middle of the Mackenzie Delta was abandoned more than 35 years ago when the government built Inuvik, but don't tell that to the 700 Dene and Inuvialuit who call Aklavik, 58 kilometers (36 miles) to the west, home. Wooden sidewalks, a legacy of Aklavik's one-time importance, link the original Hudson's Bay Company post and a mission church (now a small museum) to newer structures, built before the big move east was announced. Many large houses still stand, testimony to the fortunes made by prosperous traders in days gone by. Trails lead in all directions from town, inviting the curious to explore this small delta island.

Tours

Most people arrive in Aklavik as part of a tour from Inuvik with **Arctic Nature Tours**

(867/777-3300). On clear days, the 20-minute flight is awe-inspiring. For independent travelers, this company will arrange flights and advise on accommodation in the town's only hotel, or contact **Aklak Air** (867/777-3777, www.aklakair.ca).

TUKTOYAKTUK

Most travelers, not satisfied with driving to the end of the road, hop aboard a small plane in Inuvik for the flight along the Mackenzie Delta to Tuktoyaktuk, a small community perched precariously on an exposed gravel strip on the Beaufort Sea. Although it would be a harsh and unforgiving place to live, a visit to "Tuk," as it is sensibly known, is a delightful eye-opener. The community is spread out around **Tuktoyaktuk Harbour** and has spilled over to the gravel beach, where meter-high (three-foot) waves whipped up by cold Arctic winds roll in off the Beaufort Sea and thunder up against the shore. The most dominant natural features of the landscape are **pingos,** massive mounds of ice forced upward by the action of permafrost. The mounds look like mini-volcanoes protruding from the otherwise flat environs. The ice is camouflaged by a natural covering of tundra growth, making the pingos all the more mysterious. Approximately 1,400 pingos dot the coastal plain around Tuk, one of the world's densest concentrations of these geological wonders peculiar to the north.

Sights

Most visitors see Tuk from the inside of a transporter van driven by accommodating locals who never tire of the same hackneyed questions about living at the end of the earth. The bus stops at **Our Lady of Lourdes,** once part of a fleet of vessels that plied the Arctic delivering supplies to isolated communities. Here also are two mission churches built in the late 1930s. A stop is also made at the Arctic Ocean, where you are encouraged to dip your toes in the water or go for a swim if you really want to impress the folks back home. (Tuk is actually on the Beaufort Sea, an arm of the Arctic Ocean, but who's telling?) For a few extra bucks, you are given some time to explore on your own, including walking along the beach, climbing a nearby pingo, and checking out the well-equipped ocean port.

Practicalities

Tuk is the most popular flightseeing destination from Inuvik, and a variety of trips are offered from Inuvik. Trips start at $305, which includes the return flight (worth the price alone) and a tour of the town. The flight into Tuk is breathtaking—the pilots fly at low altitudes for the best possible views. For those who wish to spend longer in Tuk (there are enough things to do to hold your interest for at least one day), extended tours visit the community's unique cool room and include lunch with an Inuvialuit family, for $385 per person. For tour details, contact **Arctic Nature Tours** (867/777-3300). Scheduled flights are operated by **Aklak Air** (867/777-3777); accommodations are at the 18-room **Hotel Tuk Inn** (867/977-2381, $165–225 s or d).

PAULATUK

Meaning "Place of the Coal" in the local language, Paulatuk, 400 kilometers (250 miles) east of Inuvik, is a small community of 190 Inuvialuit, most of whom live a traditional lifestyle of hunting, trapping, and fishing. A Roman Catholic mission and trading post, established in 1935, attracted Inuvialuit families from camps along the Arctic coast. Their descendants continue living off the abundant natural resources. To the northeast are the **Smoking Hills,** seams of coal, rich with sulfide, that were ignited centuries ago and still burn today, filling the immediate area with distinctively shaped clouds of smoke. Sprawling across Parry Peninsula, to the east of Paulatuk, is **Tuktut Nogait National Park,** the major staging area for the 125,000-strong **bluenose caribou herd,** which migrates across the north.

Practicalities

The only accommodation in town is the **Paulatuk Visitor Centre Hotel** (867/580-3051, $185 pp), with 10 rooms that share bathrooms and a small kitchen. The only scheduled flights to Paulatuk are with **Aklak Air** (867/777-3777, www.aklakair.ca) from Inuvik. This company also does plane charters into the nearby park; or contact the Paulatuk Community Corporation (867/580-3601) for boat access.

BANKS ISLAND

Banks Island is one of the best places in the world for viewing musk oxen. Approximately 60,000 (half the world's population and the largest concentration) of these shaggy beasts call the island's **Aulavik National Park** home. Separated from the mainland by **Amundsen Gulf,** Banks is the most westerly island in the Canadian Arctic archipelago. Throughout the barren, low, rolling hills that characterize this island flow some major rivers, including the **Thomsen,** the northernmost navigable river in Canada.

Sachs Harbour (Ikaahuk)

The only permanent settlement on Banks Island is Sachs Harbour (population 150), at the foot of a low bluff along the southwest coast, 520 kilometers (323 miles) northeast of Inuvik. The town has no restaurants, only a small co-op grocery store (closed Sun.). **Aklak Air** (867/777-3777) has a twice-weekly scheduled flight to Sachs Harbour from Inuvik.

ULUKHAKTOK

Most of **Victoria Island,** separated by the Prince of Wales Strait from Banks Island, falls within Nunavut. The exception is the island's western corner, including Diamond Jenness Peninsula, where the community of Ulukhaktok (population 360) lies. Formerly known as Holman, homes here sit behind a gravel beach at the end of horseshoe-shaped Queens Bay and are surrounded by steep bluffs that rise as high as 200 meters (660 feet). The village was founded around a Hudson's Bay Company post in 1939. Inuit that moved to the post were taught printmaking by a missionary, Reverend Henri Tardi, and to this day printmaking is a major source of income for the community. Ulukhaktok also has a golf course, the northernmost in the world. Playing a round of golf here is really something to tell the folks back at the country club; for the record, the course is at a latitude of 70'44' North. In mid-July, the course hosts the **Billy Joss Open** (867/396-3080), attracting entrants from as far away as the United States.

Practicalities

Ulukhaktok's only hotel is the **Arctic Char Inn** (867/396-3501, www.arcticcharinn.com, $219 pp includes meals). Scheduled flights into Ulukhaktok are three times weekly from Yellowknife with **First Air** (867/396-3063). **Whitney & Smith** (403/678-3052, www.legendaryex.com) is a highly respected adventure tour company that includes at least one canoeing trip annually down the Thomsen River.

www.moon.com

DESTINATIONS | ACTIVITIES | BLOGS | MAPS | BOOKS

MOON.COM is ready to help plan your next trip! Filled with fresh trip ideas and strategies, author interviews, informative travel blogs, a detailed map library, and descriptions of all the Moon guidebooks, Moon.com is all you need to get out and explore the world—or even places in your own backyard. While at Moon.com, sign up for our monthly e-newsletter for updates on new releases, travel tips, and expert advice from our on-the-go Moon authors. As always, when you travel with Moon, expect an experience that is uncommon and truly unique.

MOON IS ON FACEBOOK—BECOME A FAN!
JOIN THE MOON PHOTO GROUP ON FLICKR

MAP SYMBOLS

▦ Expressway	◖ Highlight	✗ Airfield	⅃ Golf Course
Primary Road	○ City/Town	✈ Airport	℗ Parking Area
Secondary Road	◉ State Capital	▲ Mountain	≜ Archaeological Site
☐☐☐ Unpaved Road	⊛ National Capital	✚ Unique Natural Feature	♠ Church
------ Trail	★ Point of Interest		
··········· Ferry	• Accommodation	≈ Waterfall	▤ Gas Station
╍╍╍ Railroad	▼ Restaurant/Bar	▲ Park	◌ Glacier
Pedestrian Walkway	▪ Other Location		Mangrove
▥ Stairs	∧ Campground	✗ Skiing Area	Reef
		➊ Trailhead	Swamp

CONVERSION TABLES

°C = (°F – 32) / 1.8
°F = (°C x 1.8) + 32
1 inch = 2.54 centimeters (cm)
1 foot = 0.304 meters (m)
1 yard = 0.914 meters
1 mile = 1.6093 kilometers (km)
1 km = 0.6214 miles
1 fathom = 1.8288 m
1 chain = 20.1168 m
1 furlong = 201.168 m
1 acre = 0.4047 hectares
1 sq km = 100 hectares
1 sq mile = 2.59 square km
1 ounce = 28.35 grams
1 pound = 0.4536 kilograms
1 short ton = 0.90718 metric ton
1 short ton = 2,000 pounds
1 long ton = 1.016 metric tons
1 long ton = 2,240 pounds
1 metric ton = 1,000 kilograms
1 quart = 0.94635 liters
1 US gallon = 3.7854 liters
1 Imperial gallon = 4.5459 liters
1 nautical mile = 1.852 km

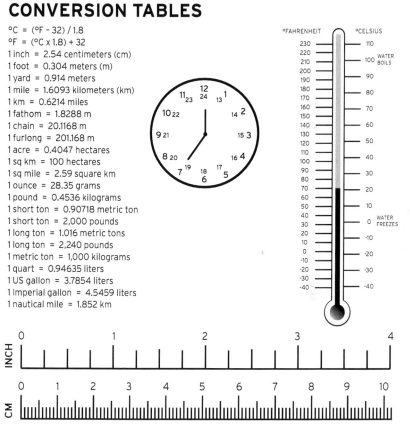

MOON THE YUKON & NORTHWEST TERRITORIES
Avalon Travel
a member of the Perseus Books Group
1700 Fourth Street
Berkeley, CA 94710, USA
www.moon.com

Editor: Shaharazade Husain
Series Manager: Kathryn Ettinger
Copy Editor: Jehan Seirafi
Graphics and Production Coordinator:
   Elizabeth Jang
Cover Designer: Elizabeth Jang
Map Editor: Albert Angulo
Cartographers: Kat Bennett, Albert Angulo

ISBN: 978-1-59880-555-0

Front cover photo: A calcite-laden creek contrasts
with the vibrant autumn color of the central Yukon
Territory near the North Klondike River Valley.
© Timothy Epp/Dreamstime.com
Title page: crooked old buildings in historic Dawson
City © Brian Scantlebury/123rf.com

Printed in the United States of America

ABOUT THE AUTHOR

Andrew Hempstead

© DIANNE MELTON

As a travel writer and photographer, Andrew Hempstead has spent many years exploring, photographing, and writing about Canada. He looks forward to spending every second summer at home in the Canadian Rockies, traveling mountain highways and hiking trails, exploring new places and updating old favorites. He spends as much time as possible on the road, traveling incognito, experiencing the many and varied delights of the region just as his readers do.

Andrew has been writing since the late 1980s, when he left an established career in advertising and took off for Alaska, linking up with veteran travel writer Deke Castleman to research and update the fourth edition of the Moon Handbook to Alaska and the Yukon. Since then he has produced several guides to Canada, including guidebooks to British Columbia, Vancouver and Victoria, Alberta, Western Canada, Atlantic Canada, and Nova Scotia. He is also the author of Moon guidebooks to Australia and New Zealand, and a contributor to *Moon San Juan Islands, Road Trip USA, Northwest Best Places*, and *Eyewitness Guide to the USA*, as well as the updater of *The Illustrated Guide to New Zealand*. His writing and photographs have appeared in a wide variety of other media, including *National Geographic Traveler, Travesias, Where, Interval World*, Microsoft's *Automap*, and on the Alaska Airlines and Expedia websites.

The website www.westerncanadatravel.com showcases Andrew's work, while also providing invaluable planning tips for travelers heading to Canada.